CW01308048

DUOLOGY – MY 30 YEARS AS AN ALCOHOLIC

(From Addiction to Redemption and Everything In-between)

1) "Desperately Seeking Sex & Sobriety"
2) "My Final Journey with Alcoholism"

Paul Pisces

DESPERATELY SEEKING SEX AND SOBRIETY

Paul Pisces

Text Copyright © Paul Pisces 2004

All rights reserved. No part of this publication may be reproduced, stored in a retrieval system, or transmitted in any form or by any means, electronic, mechanical, photocopy, recording or otherwise, without prior written permission of the copyright owner. Nor can it be circulated in any form of binding or cover other than that in which it is published and without similar condition including this condition being imposed on a subsequent purchaser.

This book is also available in paperback ISBN 0-7552-0114-0

Paul Pisces is a Piscean and likes this description found of them in the "Daily Express" (1st March 1993):

"Vague, sometimes downright evasive, sympathetic, sensitive, hugely imaginative - these are rare creatures who need careful handling otherwise they can disappear in a puff of smoke. SomePisceans are ghost-like creatures, some are voracious sharks. However, both are so emotional that they seek solace in day-dreams or addictive escape routes, whether it's music and the movies or drink and drugs. Real life is a problem because it is not like their fantasies so they can seem remote, not relating at all. With care and protection, though, they are sweet compassionate people who will adapt to your every need."

He is the product of a Grammar School education after which he studied Biology at the University of London. By the time he left university he already had a drink problem. Paul started a career in computer programming but his drinking became progressively worse and worse. Maybe you can learn something from his story.

I had it all. Fast cars, fast women, money and fame. Then I read this book. It changed my life forever. Unfortunately. - *Robert Downey (rdowney@penitentiary.com).*

Hi paul read your dsss, it was bloody great mate! i for one understood what you were on about, you sure have a way with words! you have a literary talent! keep strong mate! regards -*Anonymous.*

I am Sober also....it is really hard though. I wanted to let ya know you are not alone Buddy. Thanks for the stories. - *John.*

A sobering read (if that isn't a contradiction in terms!) I have also needed 1/3 of a bottle of vodka for breakfast and a full hip flask to keep me alive till lunch. I know how it feels and what it can do to you. I like you eventually regained some control, much of that thanks to a good woman, but I live on the edge of the abyss to this day and the possibility of falling over it is ever present. Thanks for sharing (as they say in AA). - *Graham.*

I just finished the book. It really got to me man. I have spent drunken days in the Philippines. Bar girls and booze have been my reality for a long time. I don't think you can fully recover from it. Who wants to? - *Anonymous.*

Darkly optimistic. I liked it. - *Mickey.*

I have read your book three times now and it is excellent. You need to get it published. -*Anonymous.*

good luck, paul. i much enjoyed reading your story. - *Don.*

This is the funniest satirical expose of modern life that I have read. You are either a genius or completely insane. The problem is I just can't decide which. - *Ernest Hemingway.*

Smells like teen spirit to me...... - *Kurt Cobain.*

lol i go to CRGS 6th form at the moment. How things have changed now, although you may be very pleased to know, Mr Beatty is still here!! He's such a cool teacher. The stresses of the AS levels and the pressure throughout the year nowadays is tremendous, there is very little time to get to know the teachers very well, and it seems that life is rushed. I assume you would have known Mr Rizbaf and Mr Crickmore? Who did you have for Chemistry then? Mr Evans? - *Anonymous.*

To the poster of the message above: Thanks for the message you sent - unfortunately the email address you gave is unrecognised. It's good to hear that Mr. Beatty is still at CRGS - give him my regards. I don't know Mr. Rizbaf or Mr. Crickmore - I left in the late 1970s. My Chemistry teacher was Mr. Stebbings. I can't remember who taught me Geology - I'd have to look it up. Good luck with your exams. - *Paul Pisces.*

thanatos beats eros -*Anonymous.*

And more much more than this, You did it your way. - *Sid Vicious.*

Your stuff is dark - not Joseph Heller sarcasm dark, but brutally, bare bones, reality dark. And its good. - *Dave.*

Paul, I liked your book. I enjoyed hearing about your experiences in the Philippines and also in the bay area. It reminds me of the dot com times when we all thought we were going to get rich. I also got into some trouble with drugs (Codeine), but it looks like I escaped from the problem. I just spent six months in Bangkok. I am planning to go back and live there in a couple of months. Maybe someday we will meet in South East Asia. I have burned out pretty badly here in the bay area. Work is hard to find now. It is a good time to take off. - *Silicon Valley Nerd who likes South East Asia.*

Paul, Read your book with interest, I am married to a Filipina, and unfortunately drink too much, been over there many times, your stories ring so true, made me cry, you touched a nerve mate.......take care. - *Paul.*

Brilliant. - *TJ.*

A searing indictment of the neoteric segmentation of the 'clockwork orange'. Or maybe just a good story! - *JayDee.*

I hugely enjoyed your book. I admire the brevity of your style. I shall watch out for anything else you do. - *Michael.*

The most important thing about a book is that you do not want to stop reading it. I read your book without stopping, so I reckon one day it will be published. It is so accurate, it really exposed your 'commando course of the soul' throughout. Your descriptions of the Philippines and Thailand are spot on. Perhaps the publishers of those best selling books in Thailand called Money Number 1 and Patpong on Steroids would publish your book specifically for sale in Pattaya. I am sure it would be a success. Good luck, and thanks for a great read! - *Calvin.*

Oh Lord, Where did the feeling go? Oh Lord, I never felt so low. "Chance", Stuart Adamson (Big Country) -*Anonymous.*

Just like me you're a cult. Is that the word? - *Jimi Hendrix.*

I saw the name of my school in the google search listings and took a look. I haven't read all of your book, but so far it seems really good. And you mention good ol' Mr Beatty - the school is trying to take away his animals! He is fighting them all the way though. Did you have Mr Bayes, Mr Chester or Mr Wright? They've been there for years... - *Chris.*

Roger Beatty is one of the best Biology teachers on the planet. Pete Chester taught me Geology and Roger Bayes taught me English so blame him for spelling, grammar and punctuation errors - both these guys are great teachers. - *Paul Pisces.*

What's up bro? I read and enjoyed the book and certainly identified with it. I puked my guts out this morning but I'm sure I'll be drunk again by this afternoon. Anyway, good book, cool website and the pics of boobs don't hurt either. - *Anonymous.*

I found your work on the internet because I was researching sex tourism for an anti-globalization paper. I find your vile story a prime example of the patriarchal hegemony that forces women into prostitution. Your audacity in publishing so horrendous a book on the internet is symbolic of how globalization degrades and marginalizes women all over the planet. - *A graduate student at University of South Florida.*

In reply to the comments of "A graduate student": I agree with your criticism of "patriarchal hegemony", but I think your criticism of the Book is inaccurate. I read the Book more as a warning than an endorsement of bad behaviour; Paul writes, "Don't end up a loser like me. Read this book." The Book seems to appeal more to people with alcohol problems than supporters of sex tourism. Paul, can you settle this? (In case "A graduate student" thinks I'm ignorant: I have an MA in International Studies.) Keep on writing, Paul. - *James.*

Thanks to "A graduate student" and James for your comments. The book is certainly more about alcoholism than sex tourism. I condone neither. Both are a fact of life. I will meet my maker with a clear conscience. I have done the best I could although I grant you that that wasn't very pretty. - *Paul Pisces.*

I've never been a heavy drinker, but there have been dark times in my life and I could relate to many parts of your story, a brutal tale, told with much talent. Keep banging these stories out and someone will publish you... - *darndog.*

I read your book and enjoyed it (if that's the right word). I don't have the alcohol problem you do, but I'm absolutely reckless about sex and have destroyed my life in large part because of bad decisions about it. Wife, friends and money gone. Too many prostitutes to count. If you can stop drinking you could get better, but the sex addiction doesn't go away. I've thought about the shotgun, you did a great job with that chapter. - *Charles.*

This book is dedicated to room 41 of the Swagman Narra Hotel, Angeles City, the Philippines, where most of it was written.

The website for this book can be found at:
www.paulpisces.com

In the tradition of 'Butch Cassidy and the Sundance Kid' –
"most of what follows is true……"

DESPERATELY SEEKING SEX & SOBRIETY
by Paul Pisces

Prologue
Chapter 1: Toilets & Knickers
Chapter 2: Where's Her Hole?
Chapter 3: The Once Over
Chapter 4: University Dropout
Chapter 5: Fat-Bottomed Girl
Chapter 6: Lynching Party
Chapter 7: Votes for Death
Chapter 8: Déjà vu
Chapter 9: Brothel Diversions
Chapter 10: Car Wars
Chapter 11: Farewell to Bachelorhood
Chapter 12: Cue Prologue
Chapter 13: Interview Hell
Chapter 14: Eroticism on Legs
Chapter 15: Politie
Chapter 16: Drink the Puke
Chapter 17: Blind Date
Chapter 18: Manchester Tart
Chapter 19: The Far East Calls
Chapter 20: Hello Sexy Man
Chapter 21: Fucking Crazy
Chapter 22: Consultancy Sucks
Chapter 23: San Francisco Millionaires
Chapter 24: Lady-Man
Chapter 25: Herds of Homeless
Chapter 26: New Orleans Blues
Chapter 27: Californication
Chapter 28: A Sad Story
Chapter 29: Bang, Bang, Bang
Epilogue

DESPERATELY SEEKING SEX & SOBRIETY
by Paul Pisces

Prologue

It is early afternoon and I have just left my place of work for the last time. I am a 31 year old computer specialist and I am now walking the half mile up Bergholt Road to my semi-detached house. My company car sits in the company car park and the keys are with my manager. The reality is slowly sinking in that I have been made redundant after 10 years, 1 month and 2 days service.

The two consolations are the cheque for £16,263 and the knowledge that the decision to make me redundant has probably significantly increased my life expectancy. I say this because I am an alcoholic and the amount I am currently drinking is certainly verging on the life-threatening. Prior to this event, the only possible method I had to reduce my drinking was to jack the job in. Instead the job has jacked me in. Thank God.

My calculations indicate that after I pay off my debts the money I've got should last me about six months, especially if I can reduce my alcohol intake, but following that I will be in very real trouble. Maybe by some miracle I can find another job - one must live in hope.

Alcoholism is an almost acceptable form of drug abuse which consumes you physically and mentally until you can no longer find ways to hide your problem. In my case oblivion was beginning to loom ahead of me but for this most fortunate of misfortunes.

Chapter 1: Toilets and Knickers

I have my first drink when I am a rather inexperienced 16 year old. For the last thirteen years I have been living with my parents and two brothers in a village on the outskirts of Colchester and I have recently joined a local youth club in the town. At the club I find that once the evening disco starts most of the lads mosey up East Hill to a pub called 'The Sun' (which is alas no more). The landlord has a reasonably flexible approach to the licensing laws and you can usually get a drink even if you are only knee high to a grasshopper.

As it is my first time in the boozer, I let a rather bolder, taller and more experienced lad order first. Then it is my turn.

"What'll you have?" asks the landlord.

"A half," I reply confidently.

"Yes, but what of?"

"Beer," I suggest, but with rather less confidence.

"Lager or bitter?" demands the landlord.

I order bitter and hope no-one noticed my gaffe.

After this success I proceed to pints and even spirits in the weekly binges. After a visit to the pub, the disco is a lot less daunting. I might even progress to asking a bird for a dance eventually, but let's not rush things.

In the lounge bar of 'The Sun', I am able to pick up all sorts of useful tips. For example, a very popular drink with many of the underage crowd is vodka and coke. I think it tastes pretty awful but apparently the alcohol in this drink is virtually undetectable if a police officer should just happen to make one of his unscheduled visits. At least this is what I am reliably informed. Is this the start of my slide into surreptitious drinking?

Vodka and coke quickly becomes my firm favourite as I sit quietly at a corner table of the lounge bar desperately hoping that an officer of the law won't appear to interrupt my furtive sipping. At the same time I religiously practice ordering alcoholic beverages in a particularly deep-sounding voice - God, hasn't my voice broken yet? I'm sixteen for Christ's sake. Perhaps it has - it's all the not knowing that's so worrying.

I continue studying A-level Biology, Chemistry and Geology at Colchester Royal Grammar School (which at this time is depressingly an all-boys school) with at least a modicum of success. The incredibly good news this year is that I have become one of the three part-time Biology lab stewards (thanks to good old Roger Beatty - my Biology teacher). With the money I receive from the Council for tending the school boa constrictor and other creatures of rather less distinction, I purchase a second-hand yellow Yamaha FS1E 50cc moped (known ubiquitously as a FIZZY). This allows me to attain a serious amount of independence from my parents, despite their judgment that I will probably kill myself. I nearly do. Several times.

However, now suitably endowed with a not entirely insubstantial method of propulsion, I am in a position to capitalise upon my new found, alcohol inspired confidence and my abnormal sense of humour. I've always thought I was slightly abnormal ever since I was eight and used to fantazise about tying up mature young ladies (a contradiction in terms that I concede) in order to subject them to encounters with spiders and the like. But there again, men are basically peculiar beasts and a male human with a vivid imagination can be a very peculiar being indeed.

Deep thoughts of any substance have not really surfaced in my confused psyche at this point but I am fascinated by all things scientific and anything to do with toilets and knickers.

Going up the boozer of a Thursday night is still an interesting experience and some of the blokes I know have even managed to pull birds (with tits). I, unfortunately, remain an ornithologist; watching tits in great detail but not actually handling any.

But, joy of joys, after many unsuccessful forays into the disco dancing throng, once the slow dances have started, with a polite, "Excuse me would you like to dance?" I eventually begin getting the occasional acceptance.

Since that time I have learned of some rather more unusual opening gambits. One of my favourites is, "Can I kiss your pussy?" Or for the really dangerously ambitious, "Do you take it up the arse, darling?" However, for those interested, the most reliable opening gambit is thought to be, "Can I buy you a large drink?" After a lot to drink there is a temptation to use the rather less successful,

"Would you like to buy me a large drink, love?" but this approach should generally be avoided.

Once on the dance floor with the girl, preferably vertical in the early stages, the idea is to manoeuvre the hands toward the buttock area and you can monitor your potential by how far towards the buttocks the hands are allowed. I always favour the right hand lead nestling in the small of the back, followed by the unobtrusive buttock stroke to gauge the resistance of the opposing forces. Needless to say, a double handed-buttock clench is a dead cert.

The problem arising at this stage is that of nonchalant, confident conversation with a member of the opposite sex without getting a hard-on. After several not very substantial conversations on what flavour gum the girl is chewing, I decide to do some homework.

In many respects I am lucky because I go to a good school and have got a good grounding in the art of study. This means that when I decide I need to study the art of conversation, I am familiar with the process of how to go about it and I am confident that I will succeed, eventually, in gaining a reasonable understanding of what is required. Learning anything is a process. It can be defined in a nutshell as follows:

1) Decide what you need to know.
2) Read and study the available resources.
3) Formulate your hypotheses.
4) Test your hypotheses in the real world.

I happen upon a pretty old text (even at this time) called 'How To Win Friends And Influence People' by Dale Carnegie. I think it was written in the fifties for budding sales executives but there is some useful stuff in it. The most memorable is his assertion that conversation often works best if you talk about or show interest in the other person's interests or problems. Simple really but it works. This isn't necessarily a recipe for smooth talking or conning people (it can be) but if you are genuinely interested in someone then you should show it in your conversation.

One thing I discover from using this technique is that some of the girls I am physically attracted to, I am not compatible with emotionally or intellectually. Relationships based purely on physical attraction are normally doomed to be short-lived.

My school years are a success of sorts. I end up with three 'A' levels: Biology, Chemistry and Geology.

My school report contains the following:

Chemistry:

"Both in written work and orally is inclined to be superficial at times."

Geology:

"The level of his comments in class is still very superficial."

Biology:

"Excellent. Considerable promise for the future. Well done."

(Good old Roger Beatty!)

Form master:

"Progressing well though hardly to Oxbridge standard."

University beckons. Well, it beats working, especially when you don't know what you want to do. Oxbridge is out (see comment above). Veterinary school is out, so is medicine (results not good enough). Research in biochemistry could be fun. You know; DNA, the double helix, Watson & Crick. Go for it.

Chapter 2: Where's Her Hole?

I load my aging purple mini (I had upgraded my moped the year before) with virtually every belonging I own. There is barely room for me to squeeze into the driving seat. I can hardly see out of the back window in the rear view mirror. Do I really need all this? Well 'be prepared' was our cub scout motto and prepared I am going to be.

I am 18 and leaving home for the first time to live in London. For an insecure country boy, this is a daunting challenge and I am quite apprehensive.

I picked Westfield College, which is part of the University of London, because you can live on campus for at least 2 of the 3 years, it has a good reputation for biochemistry and, if everything goes pear-shaped, I can rush home to mum and dad in about 2 hours.

After the drive down to the college, I finally collect the key to the room I am to share with a complete stranger. As I approach the room, the door is ajar and I can hear noises coming from inside. It is apparent that my room-mate has already arrived. He seems friendly enough and he is clearly a bit of a lad.

"Hi, my name's Mark. Hey, you don't mind if my girlfriend comes to stay do you? We won't disturb you. I'll tell her not to moan too loudly."

"Well, I suppose..."

"You've got a girlfriend have you?"

"Er no, not at the moment."

"You have had a girl though?"

"Yes, of course."

"Where's a girl's cunt then?" he asks smiling.

"What do you mean?"

"Where's her hole, show me."

I point to my crotch.

"Na, na it's not there - it's underneath innit, you know, under there."

I move my finger further down.

"Yes, yes that's where I meant," I confirm enthusiastically.

"Don't worry," Mark reassures me, "I'll tell my girl not to bother to visit......unless I get desperate."

"Yeah right, whatever you say."

Mark has arrived with a small rucksack and appears to me to be very unprepared.

"Have you got much stuff?" he inquires. "Do you want a hand?"

We go to the car and his eyes boggle at the amount of gear I've brought.

Surprisingly enough we get on well (he is another biochemistry undergraduate) and our "gang" is soon joined by two more biochemists. Marcus is a friend of Mark's from school and Paul is a quiet, shy guy I befriend at a lecture. Or does he befriend me? (I am quiet and shy too - unless I'm drunk). Marcus is a giant. I am 6 feet tall, as is Mark, and Marcus towers above us. He must be 6'4" or thereabouts. Paul reminds me a bit of Bruce Springsteen. He is shorter (5'10") but well-built and brawny. I am the thinnest, only 10 stone (140 lbs) but reasonably fit by which I mean I can clean and jerk my body weight over my head on a good day.

My new pals are impressed because I have a car and I am impressed because they seem more knowledgeable about life than me. Mark seems especially knowledgeable.

The car means we can easily get to parties at other colleges in London. The bad news is that I have to drive.

"You've just overtaken a plain clothes police car!" Mark exclaims.

"Are you sure?" I splutter, quickly taking the plastic beer glass away from my lips.

"Yeah, the coppers were in uniform."

"Damn! Get rid of this beer, Mark."

We are well ahead of the police car by now, so Mark opens the mini window and throws our four beers over some railings. I slow down.

The police car overtakes and flags me down. An officer walks over and indicates for me to get out. Oh dear! The driver's door is broken. I nudge Mark and he climbs out the passenger door. I slide over the passenger seat and out the same door. It doesn't look good.

"Evening Sir. Could you tell me what speed you were doing as you overtook us?" the officer inquires.

"About 45 miles an hour," I admit sheepishly.

"And what is the speed limit in this area, Sir?"

"30?" I suggest.

"Yes Sir. You were at least 15 miles an hour over the speed limit."

"Sorry, Officer." I look remorseful. I am quite good at looking remorseful.

Life tip: Always look remorseful when caught bang to rights by the cops.

"Well Sir, we'll let you off tonight with a warning but be more responsible in the future."

"Thank you Officer. I certainly will."

The officer returns to the police car which quickly pulls away into the busy London traffic.

Yes, yes, yes! They must be too busy to worry about remorseful me. Did they see the beer? I don't know. It doesn't matter now - we escaped! (Correction: I escaped. I was the only one in trouble unless they got Mark for destroying evidence.) Off to the party!

Partying by now is a much more sophisticated affair than the youth club disco. We look cool (coolish). We drink either lager or barley wine (ugh). We know the form. Well, Mark does.

The party is in full swing when we arrive, with a talented reggae band kicking out some Bob Marley. With the barley wine coursing through my veins I am flying. After a while I spot a likely-looking girl and make my move. I forego my tried and trusted opening gambit of, "Can I buy you a large drink?" and instead say, "Hello. Is this your college? I'm here with some friends from Westfield." Anyway things progress well. I decide to have another beer.

In order to create a dance floor, the low-backed padded lounge chairs which normally occupy the room have been placed against the wall with their backs toward the dance floor. This creates a comfy place to rest, lolling with your bottom propped up on the back of the chair.

"Are you free tomorrow night?" I ask while slipping my arm around the girl's shoulders. I'm feeling a bit light-headed now and my coordination is giving me a few problems.

"I'm not sure. Perhaps I could give you my phone number." The girl is still sizing me up.

Yes, yes, yes! We're in. Just stay cool, take it easy and we're on our way. I decide to take another gulp of beer. It's a bad mistake.

As my hand comes up, my foot slips. I lose my balance and find myself falling backwards onto the seat of the chair, the contents of my beer glass follow me. As I come to rest sprawled across the seats and half-hidden by the chair backs, I can see the prize I had worked so hard to win disappearing into the distance…..

The first year continues with rounds of lectures, parties, drinking and finally exams. We view the list of passes posted on the college notice board expectantly, desperately hoping our names are there. Actually we are all just hoping our own name is there. Fuck the others! God is smiling on us and we are all destined to survive to year 2. After a round of hearty congratulations and celebrations we all disperse for the holidays.

Chapter 3: The Once Over

During the holidays I spend a lot of time with my old mate from school, Glen. It was Glen who got me to join the youth club and it was Glen who showed me the ropes. He is a guy with a heart of gold and I promise that I have forgiven him for shooting at me with that air pistol.

By this time the fact that he shot at me with an air pistol is ancient history. I have virtually forgotten about it. And I have definitely forgiven him. Honest. Glad we could clear that up. I met Glen when we were 15 and it wasn't until we were 16 that he shot at me with an air pistol. I won't mention it again.

But now we are both 19 and it's the holidays. Yippee! Glen has a girlfriend (Elaine - now his wife) but that doesn't stop us racing round town and whooping it up at either the nightclub in Eld Lane (The Affair - alas no more) or the club behind the Siege House pub (L'Aristos). Sometimes, just for a change, we go to Essex University on the edge of Colchester if there is a good band playing.

It is at a gig at the university that I meet Louisa. Glen and I are standing on the fringe of the dancing melee, beer in hand, eyeing the talent when suddenly Glen exclaims, "Come on. There's a girl I know over there. It's Louisa. I'll introduce you."

Glen leads me towards the far wall where an astonishingly pretty girl stands alone. She has long, fine, naturally blonde hair parted in the middle, full lips with bright red lipstick and innocent but friendly blue eyes. I am captivated. Glen makes chit-chat as I stare hypnotised by this girl's beauty.

"This is Paul," announces Glen and he elbows me to get my attention. I do my best to make conversation while Glen goes to get us all another drink. I ask her how she knows Glen - she used to live in the same street. What does she do? She's going to go to teacher training college in Chichester on the south coast after the holidays. I am just babbling. Anything to stay in the presence of this goddess.

Glen returns with the drinks. More chit-chat. Glen is good at chit-chat. He's a natural. Open, friendly, warm. A good guy. One of the best. Louisa says she's got to go as her lift is due. "Can I ring you?" I mumble. Did I really say it or did I imagine it? She opens her handbag, pulls out an eyeliner, writes her number down on a scrap of paper and hands it to me. I did say it! I did say it! Yes, yes, yes. I've got her fucking number. There is a God! Holy fuck! There is a God!

After a few stiff drinks to calm the nerves, I ring Louisa the next evening and manage to arrange a date for the following night. I tell her that I have heard there's another gig at the university so that's where we decide to go.

I pick her up and am given the once over by her mum. I think I pass. Louisa looks fantastic and I get a hard-on but fortunately this fact is not registered by her mum. If I were to be hyper-critical, Louisa has smallish breasts (which in fact I like) and a slightly big arse but in the tight black cords she's wearing, I wouldn't change a thing. We make small-talk about school, college, her brother, my brothers. It's all going well until we arrive at the university. The bands play down in the basement and as we go down the stairs it is all quiet and very obvious that there is no gig. Louisa looks nervous.

"Its OK," I say. "We must have got the wrong night. Let's go to the uni bar."

She looks relieved and smiles.

In the bar we drink and chat. Her parents divorced several years ago and her mum has a steady boyfriend who's a good guy by all accounts. The Sex Pistols blare out of the juke box. She tells me that she is 18.

"What star-sign are you?" I ask. (Well you have to don't you?)

"Pisces," she smiles. (God, she looks sexy when she smiles).

"That's a coincidence. I'm a Piscean too. When is your birthday?"

"March 18th," she says.

My mouth drops open.

"That's my birthday!" I shout.

What a coincidence. This is fate. We both realise it. The ice is broken. We laugh and hug. A drunk student comes over to our table and slurs that it's nice to see two people in love. Too many sad people in the world he continues. (I always attract odd people. Drunks, loonies, losers, they all want to talk to me. Worrying isn't it?) Louisa is relaxed and happy and the drunk leaves us winking and smiling.

"You know, I was really worried earlier," she confides.

"When?" I ask, happy because she now wants to confide in me. We are practically an item.

"In the basement. I thought you might be a rapist."

We both laugh. The ice is completely melted. I'm not a rapist. It's official. All barriers are down. I think we are an item.

I drop her off at home where we kiss and fondle. We are, after all, an item. I drive away happier than I can ever remember.

Yes, yes, yes. I have a girlfriend. There is a God. There must be.

Later in the holidays I am invited to a party by our rich neighbour's daughter. I had recently met up with Sarah in London, before I met Louisa, and I had a bit of a crush on her. It was an unrequited love.

The party is quite a lavish affair and the champagne is flowing freely. I am able to take Louisa and she is suitably impressed. My parents are away on holiday and my mind is working overtime.

Midnight arrives and the party is beginning to wind down. Louisa (Lou) and I make our excuses and I quietly suggest to her that she might like to stay the night with me. Rather unexpectedly she agrees but says she'll have to ring her mum. She can ring the bloody Archbishop of Canterbury for all I care. Yes, yes, yes!

We walk to my parents' house hand in hand. It is a beautiful summer night. The stars are out. Surely a fuck isn't out of the question. Inside, Lou rings her mum but she's on the phone a long time and I begin to sweat. Fifteen minutes later all appears to be resolved. Parental approval or at least acceptance has been obtained. But for what?

We go upstairs to my parents' room and undress. Lou tells me she's a virgin. I had guessed this. What she hasn't guessed is that I'm a virgin too. It's the blind leading the blind. God help us! Fortunately I've read and reread 'The Joy of Sex' and 'More Joy of Sex' so I'm hopeful that my foreplay is up to the job. Plus I know where her cunt is because Mark told me. It's underneath.

God, a virgin fucking a virgin is hard work but eventually we get it in. It is actually quite good fun and I think we are both very relieved not to be virgins anymore. We cuddle and kiss and sleep.

In the morning, nursing our hangovers, we wash the bedsheets. Blood everywhere. That's virgins for you. I take her home. We are in love, you cynics. It's official.

Chapter 4: University Dropout

I arrive the day before the first day of term and make my way to the college's accommodation office because I have heard a rumour that some rooms might be available for 2nd year students. No luck.

I enter the student bar and find the other guys sitting drinking. Unlike me they are well organised. They tell me that they arrived in London early and have already rented a small, cheap (dilapidated) 3-bedroom house and they are basically sorted. Two other second-year friends, Kim (male) and Peter, yesterday took the last college room going. Oh shit! I didn't realise it was going to be this difficult to get accommodation. The guys suggest I sleep on a couch at their house but as it's miles away I decide to bed down in a common room for the time being. Something will turn up, won't it?

After a month of this I get depressed. The courses are dull, the novelty of university has worn off and I'm fed up with sleeping in a common room. Lou is at teacher training college in Chichester and my misery is so complete that neither talking to her on the phone nor her frequent letters can cheer me up. I decide I've had enough of studying. I tell my tutor and my friends I'm leaving. I leave.

Back home with my parents I do cheer up. My older brother James is at university in London (not Westfield) reading Classical Studies (bet that will come in useful) so I get his room. My younger brother Robert is at school or out doing his Hospital Radio presenting or some such. He's no bother. The world's my oyster and I begin looking for a job.

Time passes and it begins to dawn on me. Nobody wants a university dropout. Nobody wants a failure when there is a surplus of successes. Nobody wants me. I begin to despair. I buy bottles of vodka and drink alone in my room until I get happy. (I am a happy drunk.) As I drink my mind races, looking for the way forward. After about 6 weeks, I come to the realisation that I must phone my tutor and beg to be allowed to return to university. What a humiliation.

I have a large vodka. And another. I pick up the phone and dial.

"Hello," says a voice.

"Hello. Is that Dr. Greene? It's Paul here. I left a while ago….do you remember?"

"Hello Paul. Yes of course I remember. How are you?"

"Not too good actually, Dr. Greene. I want to come back. Come back and study. Is that possible?"

Dr. Greene becomes serious.

"Well Paul, you haven't actually officially left. There's nothing in writing. You can come back anytime but you've missed a lot of work."

He sounds very neutral. Not at all encouraging. He wasn't happy I left. He was my principal lecturer and he led the second year biochemistry course.

"OK. I'll be back on Monday," I exclaim gleefully.

Yes, yes, yes! I haven't actually officially left. That's official. Whether he likes it or not I'm back in. The light at the end of the tunnel is switched back on. I have another vodka.

I drive back to London on Sunday and go and visit the guys in their dilapidated house. They have fantastic news for me because they have heard that Peter has just moved out of the room he shares with Kim to go and live with his girlfriend. This means there is a spare bed in the college.

It's 9am Monday and I report to the college accommodation officer. I tell him my story and find he is not amused.

"Why didn't you tell us earlier that you were having trouble finding accommodation?" he bellows.

Because I didn't bloody well know you'd do anything about it, I think to myself while looking remorseful. He explains that the room Kim is in is supposed to be a guest room for visitors to the college and not student accommodation. I look very remorseful indeed.

"All right, since Kim is already in the room you might as well have the spare bed."

Yes, yes, yes! I am saved. The Red Sea has parted and the Israelites can move forward. A resounding success.

I find Kim in our room listening to a tape of the Police. "Can't stand losing you" is echoing off the walls and down the corridor. The room is a bit bigger and better appointed than the normal student rooms and there is a bathroom and toilet directly opposite the door. Kim turns the volume down on his cassette player and I throw the bags I am carrying onto the unoccupied bed.

"Hi Kim, hope you don't mind getting a new roommate."

"No, that's fine," says Kim. "I was a bit worried that with Peter gone the college might pressure me to move out. You do know this is really a guest room."

"Yeah, they told me."

Kim's a good bloke, a bit like Paul but even quieter. By lucky chance he's another biochemist (they're everywhere at Westfield) and we get on fine. Over the next few weeks he helps me to try and catch up on all the work I've missed. I start to relax and begin to pine for Louisa.

Chapter 5: Fat-Bottomed Girl

By the second term of the second year I am back in a routine of sorts although I am still worried about all the work I missed. Life is still the normal hectic round of parties and lectures with the emphasis on parties. I have a nagging disquiet in the back of my mind, however, because the exams are not so very far away and they are going to be much tougher than last year. I manage to ignore this nagging doubt for the moment and decide that since everything is going so well, I will drive to Chichester and visit Louisa for the weekend. It's a long drive but I'm sure the car can make it.

I ring Louisa to gauge her reaction and she is very enthusiastic. She mentions something about me having to sleep in a common room but I am sure she is joking. She better be joking because I am as horny as a warren full of rabbits.

I leave after lectures on Friday night. It's getting dark and it's raining as I navigate from north London where my college is to south London in order to get on the main road going south. Chichester is located on the south coast of England.

The rush hour traffic is bad and progress is slow. 'Fat-Bottomed Girls' by Queen is booming from the radio and I'm singing along and feeling great. In a few hours I will be with my very own fat-bottomed girl and hopefully I'll be in her bed. Then I notice that the car is handling very badly. I park as best I can considering the narrow road and the nose-to-tail traffic and, sliding over the passenger seat as usual, I emerge into heavy rain. It is immediately apparent what the problem is: I have a puncture. Damn!

It takes ages to change the tyre and now I have no spare wheel, I am soaking wet, I am tired and I am late. The roads are quieter by now so in order to try and make up some time I put my foot down and am speeding along when I notice I've nearly passed the turn off to get on the main road south. I glance in the rear view mirror and decide it's safe to make a last-minute, high-speed maneuver. As I make the turn I hear a desperate honking and a screeching of brakes. I automatically hit the brakes too and the car skids dangerously, coming to a halt just before the embankment marking the intersection of the two roads. The other car has come to a halt almost level with me but on the left hand side of the road. The driver of the other car gets out and I do likewise. He is cursing.

"What the hell are you doing? You nearly killed both of us!"

"Sorry," I say and look remorseful. "I didn't see you, you must have been in my blind spot."

"Jesus!" says the man. "OK, OK. It could have been your blind spot." He calms down a bit. "No harm done, I suppose. Are you all right?"

"Yes thanks," I say. "Look, I'm really sorry. It was my fault."

Life tip: In life if it's your fault put your hand up and take the blame. Nobody's perfect.

The man has now calmed down and, getting back in his car, he drives off with a wave.

I continue to Chichester driving more slowly and I arrive safely but very late at the large block of student rooms where Louisa is a resident. She is still up when I ring her from a nearby phone box and she collects me from the main entrance and takes me to her room. She has put her nickname 'Lou' on the door in big letters. How cute, I think to myself. We sleep close together in her small single bed but we are both very tired. The rabbits in the warren will have to wait.

We wake up late and we both seem to have the same thing on our mind. There is quite a bit of noise outside in the corridor as the other residents move about getting their breakfast. After a bit of cunnilingus, Lou gets on top of me and starts moving her hips in a slow, sensual rhythm. It's heaven. I am licking her nipples with the end of my tongue and she is making a low moaning sound with her eyes closed. Suddenly the door bursts open and a well-dressed, well-built woman in her fifties is standing before me. Lou turns and looks over her shoulder at the astonished woman. All three of us are startled and in a state of shock. After what seems an eternity the woman mumbles "Sorry", fumbles for the door handle and leaves us. We look at each other and then begin shrieking hysterically.

Subsequently Lou talks to her friends and discovers that this woman is the mother of one of the residents, here for a visit with her daughter. She needed the bathroom and while walking down the corridor she saw 'Lou' on the door and mistook it for 'Loo'. Louisa had neglected to lock her room door.

The rest of the weekend passes quickly as Louisa takes me on a whirlwind tour of her college and introduces me to her friends. There are so many girls here I begin to wish I was training to be a teacher and not wasting my time on a biochemistry degree.

Saturday night is party night and I am drunk and dancing to the Blondie album "Parallel lines". Through the fog of alcohol it suddenly strikes me that Louisa has more than a passing resemblance to Debbie Harry except with a bigger arse. I am a lucky, lucky boy.

At the end of the weekend I return to London with all my appetites fully satiated. Roll on the summer holidays.

Back at college term 2 becomes term 3 and the inevitability of the exams is unavoidable. Everyone is in a panic revising morning, afternoon, evening and night. I am concentrating especially hard on my biochemistry course because this is my major subject. I still have weak spots around some areas because of the work I missed but I decide to leave these weak areas alone and concentrate on what I know best as this does comprise the bulk of the course. This is another big mistake.

Quite soon it's exam time and I am sitting in the main examination hall waiting to turn over the biochemistry exam paper. I feel confident. I am the best prepared for any exam that I can remember and I should easily find enough questions on my good topics to sail through. Turning over the paper I read rapidly, searching for questions that I can answer. As I reach the end of the paper my heart starts pounding, my knees go weak and I realise my predicament - most of the questions focus on the parts of the syllabus I missed. Fuck! I am angry and scared at the same time - am I paranoid or have I been stitched up? Slowly I calm down and decide to get on with it, answering the questions as best I can. Maybe I can scrape a pass. I don't.

University heaven didn't last long and I am now a failure in the core subject of my degree. I am summoned to see my tutor, Dr. Greene.

"I am surprised you didn't put more effort into revising for the biochemistry exam," he says.

Wanker, I think.

"Well, I think I was a bit unlucky with the questions. I was actually very well prepared in most topics."

"That's as may be, but needless to say you can't continue with your biochemistry degree as you've failed the core course." He seems smug. "However, you have passed enough other units to continue to the 3rd year but we'll have to change your degree to Biological Sciences."

That's a relief. I thought for a moment they were going to kick me out. But this does mean that my intended career as a researcher in biochemistry has been knocked on the head. Not to worry, I'd been getting a bit sick of science anyway and something else will turn up. I hope.

Since my degree course has been broadened out for me I decide to scour the biology curriculum looking for interesting courses. 'Computer Organisation and Machine-level Programming' is one I find. Hmm, computers; that's different. I think I'll do that next year. Pays better than research, I bet.

I return home to my parents' house for the summer holidays and work as a delivery driver for Williams & Griffin, a well known department store in Colchester. The money I earn helps pay to keep my car on the road and my evenings out with Louisa. One evening she suggests we visit her grandparents for the weekend......in Carlisle.

Chapter 6: Lynching Party

Carlisle is close to Gretna Green where eloping lovers traditionally go to get married. I do hope Lou hasn't got any funny ideas.

We load our suitcases into the car as I worry about whether this old mini has any chance of getting all the way to Carlisle and back. We shall see. I am also worried about where I will be sleeping in Carlisle. Will Lou and I be sharing a bed as we often have or will we be putting on a show for the old folks?

Surprisingly we make good time in spite of some very wet weather and arrive safely at Lou's grandparents on Friday night. After a round of introductions I am shown to my room. Show for the old folks it is, worst luck.

We spend a pleasant Saturday touring round in the grandparents' car, visiting Roman emperor Hadrian's wall and other tourist attractions. By Saturday night I am feeling very horny and Louisa and I contrive to spend the evening by ourselves. Waving goodbye to the grandparents, we drive my mini to a local pub and order some drinks. I am in a lager mood tonight while Lou has her usual gin and tonic. We talk about our day, her grandparents, life in general and the future. We have always got on well ever since we met, possibly because we are both Pisceans, and I am convinced that this is the girl I will one day marry. Just not yet. She doesn't want to elope at the moment so that's a great relief and gently I move the conversation towards how horny I am. After several gin and tonics, it turns out that she's a bit horny too, so we decide to go somewhere a bit more private.

The car is parked a short distance away on a side road. It's dark, it's quiet and there's not really anyone about. We climb into the back seat of the car and begin heavy petting. She has her hands down my briefs and things are just getting interesting when a police car pulls up with its headlights beaming onto us. I can't believe it. The cops are everywhere. Having dampened our ardour and weakened my erection, they drive off.

We get back into the front seats where I have an idea.

"Let's drive further down this country lane where no-one will find us," I suggest. Lou nods her agreement. We set off and after about a mile, I pull off the road onto a wide grass verge. In the back seat the heavy petting progresses well and despite the cramped conditions I finally manage to do the business. We clean up with some paper handkerchiefs that Louisa has in her handbag and, as it's now quite late, agree to return to Lou's grandparents house.

It's begun raining again and as we transfer to the front seats of the car, for the first time it strikes me how muddy it is on this verge. We clean the mud off our shoes as best we can and I start the car. Mini's have front wheel drive and I have parked the car on the verge facing away from the road, so I put the gears into reverse and prepare to edge the car backwards. Slipping the clutch I await movement. Nothing. I check the gears and try again. Still nothing. Opening the car window, I look down and see the front wheels spinning viciously, digging a trench in the mud. Fuck! I look at Louisa.

"Houston, I think we've got a problem," I say. She giggles.

Minutes later we are both ankle deep in mud, furiously attempting to push the obstinate car onto the road. I have filled the trench cut by the spinning wheels with a few branches and the carpet from the car in the hope of providing some traction but it is to no avail. It's raining hard now and I think Lou is crying. I am caked in mud where I slipped over during my exertions. We sit in the car and rest. I admit defeat.

Life tip: Never park on muddy grass verges especially if you've got only front wheel drive.

"Look, we'll have to ring your grandparents," I say.

"But it's 2 o'clock in the morning," she wails.

"They'll still be up. They'll be worried, won't they?"

She sees the logic in this and we trudge in the rain back to the phone box by the pub.

"Where are you? We were so worried!" I can hear her grandfather ask down the phone.

"Sorry," says Lou, looking remorseful. (Maybe this is a Piscean trait.) She explains where we are and we wait huddling inside the phone box out of the rain.

A short time later the grandparents show up in their car. Granny's carrying a tow rope; at least I think it's a tow rope or maybe this is a lynching party.

"We were so worried!" they exclaim in unison.

"Sorry," we repeat together. We both look very remorseful. As we all drive together to where the mini is stuck grandmother asks, "What were you doing all the way down this little lane?" Everybody goes quiet. Even the car seems to be running more quietly. There is a deathly hush. This is a tricky question and I decide to leave it for Lou to field.

"We got lost and were trying to turn round when we got stuck," she says with as much conviction as she can muster. Brilliant! I try to keep a straight face. Under pressure this girl's good. I squeeze her hand.

It doesn't take long to tow the mini free and I finally hit the sack at 3-30 in the morning. I sleep fitfully. I'll be glad to leave tomorrow. We spend an uneventful Sunday morning and leave for Colchester after lunch. We are all smiles. It's been an interesting weekend, hasn't it?

As the holidays progress Lou and I start to have problems. She wants to go out with her friends a lot and often seems reluctant to spend time with me. I don't know what's wrong but Glen is always happy to come out for a night of drinking and disco.

One evening Glen picks me up in his old Ford Escort at about 8pm and we go to a pub in Dedham called 'The Malborough' where we drink lager and play our favourite video game, 'Galaxian'. After an hour or so of this we set off to visit a nightclub in Sible Hedingham, which we have visited once or twice before.

The disco is going full pelt by the time we arrive and at the bar we order more lager. It's Glen's round so while he pays, I find the toilet. I relieve myself and emerge keen to find Glen and my lager. Then I see her. Our eyes meet. She's wearing a bright blue jumpsuit and in her makeup she looks stunning. Sitting next to her is a balding, muscular, older guy. Louisa looks away from me and towards her new beau. Everything is suddenly clear. I find Glen, down my lager in one go and order a whisky. Better make it a double.

The next evening I ring Louisa at home. It's a teary conversation. He's a builder, she met him at a club, no she's not in love she just wants to play the field a bit. I understand, I think. What she means is……it's over.

Chapter 7: Votes for Death

All third year students at Westfield are entitled to single-room college accommodation, so I have none of the problems of last year. Kim and I choose separate rooms in the same building but Mark, the other Paul and Marcus, who have become known as the 3 musketeers, continue to share their dilapidated shack. I think they like their independence.

Mark, Paul and Marcus are all fairly heavy drinkers come the evening but I have already begun to notice that I tend to drink faster and harder than any of them, or our other friends for that matter. It's the stress, I tell myself. Once this year is out of the way and I've got my degree, I'll find a good job, earn a good living and all will be well.

Tonight we've been out to a party (what's new, you're asking) and I'm driving the 3 musketeers back to their house. We are in the last 2 or 3 miles of the journey when suddenly I shout "Votes for death! Who votes for death!" (This has become a tradition on the way back from parties.)

"Death, death, death!" scream my passengers, egging me on as I weave the car about, trying to drive as close as possible to parked cars without hitting them. The road is narrow but it is late and there is very little traffic about.

Please understand that I do not condone this behaviour - it's just what happened.

Life tip: Please do NOT try this at home.

As we approach an island in the road marking the next right-hand turn I need to make, I decide it would be a thrill to drive on the wrong side of the island. I am successful in negotiating this maneuver, much to the amusement of my passengers, but then suddenly Mark cries out.

"There's a copper in the road....he's waving a torch at us."

The policeman is obviously trying to flag us down but by the time I spot him, I've passed him and I just keep going.

"You nearly ran him over!" Mark shouts.

"No I didn't," I retort and, thinking fast, I switch off the car's lights so the copper can't read my number plate.

Back at their home, I drink cups of coffee and sweat a lot.

"Jesus! You were lucky there," Paul says.

"Lucky! You nearly killed him," Mark observes.

After an hour or so I have to make a move since I still have to get back to my room at college.

"Which way are you going back?" asks Marcus, ever the pragmatist.

"Well, the same way we came," I reply. "That's quickest."

"But the copper could still be there," Marcus persists.

"Na, he'll be long gone by now," I counter. But the others join in and eventually get me to agree to take the long way home.

"Bye," I say, waving and pulling out of their driveway. I have already made up my mind to go back the same way I came, mainly because I don't want to get lost in the maze of London streets that make up this area.

Uneventfully, I pass the site of my run-in with the law but have to stop at a set of traffic lights a few hundred yards further on. I see in my rear view mirror a large black Rover pull up behind me but I continue to concentrate on the traffic lights, waiting for them to change.

A loud knocking on the driver side window pulls me out of my trance. It's a copper! Oh no! Now I remember - a lot of plain clothes police cars are black Rovers. It's a bust! I slide over the passenger seat and climb out of the passenger door, as usual.

"Did you nearly run me over about an hour ago?" asks the policeman sarcastically.

"Er, I don't know," I mumble.

"Well, have you been drinking, Sir?" he leers.

"I had a few beers earlier," I confirm.

The copper talks into his walkie-talkie and a Black Maria arrives with more policemen.

"We'll have to take you down the nick for a breath test," says the copper.

I clamber into the back of the Black Maria and find it is full of drunken Scottish football fans. I sit quietly, resigned to my fate, as the Black Maria is driven to the local nick.

At the nick I am interviewed by a Sergeant. He is overworked and the police are plainly very busy with all the drunken Scottish fans. I am looking as remorseful as I possibly can.

"Blow into this, please Sir," says the Sergeant, handing me a tube full of crystals attached to a breathalyser bag. I blow up the bag and begin praying while the two coppers eye the tube closely as the crystals begin to turn green. There is a line on the tube and if the crystals beyond this line turn green I'm done for. The Sergeant eventually hands the tube to me for inspection.

"It's very close," he says. He is deciding whether or not to give me the benefit of the doubt.

"He nearly ran me over," the first officer interjects hoping to sway the Sergeant. I observe the tube and it is clear the crystals are green just beyond the line. But it is very close. I summon up all my skills and look the most remorseful I've ever looked in my young life.

"I am going to give you the benefit of the doubt," says the Sergeant sternly. Loud noises can be heard in the corridor outside. The Scottish football fans are probably rioting.

"Please follow this officer and collect your car from the car park." The Sergeant hurries off to quell the riot and I am left alone with a policeman I've nearly killed.

"Follow me," he says. His anger has subsided somewhat and he has accepted his Sergeant's decision.

"I'm sorry about earlier," I offer as an apology.

"Yes, well, just count yourself lucky."

"Yes I do. Thank you."

The officer hands me the keys to my car. I open the passenger door, slide over into the driver's seat and drive off carefully with my best effort at a friendly wave. Yes I do count myself lucky. Very lucky indeed. Will my luck hold? Not likely is it?

Chapter 8: Deja Vu

My degree certificate is sent to me at my parents' home and I open it without much of a fanfare. I already know the result. It's a 2nd class honours degree (lower division) in Biological Sciences. A 2:2, a so-called gentleman's degree, implying you were bright but couldn't be bothered to work. I did work, but patchily. I was excellent at some courses and bored by others. I was also drinking and partying far too much.

Mark and Paul have gone off on a tour of Africa. They both got 2:1s. Marcus was considering the possibility of becoming a policeman. I lost touch with them all. I rang Paul's home number once, much later, and his father told me he was doing biochemistry research at Oxford University and living on a canal boat. Sounds nice. I didn't follow up on it.

After a spell temping in a solicitor's office, I finally get a computer programming job working for Philips Business Systems in Colchester. I am working in the headquarter's of Philips computer business in the UK. Elektra House, as it is called, is an impressive looking building outside Colchester's mainline railway station. Just up the road is a small pub called the Bricklayer's Arms where, on a Friday lunch time, all Philips' computer programmers go to socialise. Computer programmers as a rule are not particularly sociable but the Philips' lot is a small close-knit team and quite friendly.

At this time a very rudimentary DOS-based IBM PC has only just appeared on the scene and the dominance of Windows and Microsoft is still in the future. Unix is widespread but only in academia (universities get free Unix licences). Commercial computer users in the UK buy proprietary systems from IBM or the BUNCH (Burroughs, Unisys, NCR, CDC, Honeywell). Philips is a niche player and the team in Colchester supports a system called the P6000 which focuses on the financial market.

Working on computers suits me; so long as the computer programs work properly, everyone's happy. There can, however, be a lot of stress. Deadlines are invariably tight and the technology is complex and ever-changing. I am seeing a lot of Glen again and we spend our evenings drinking hard and looking for women. After a hard night partying, I occasionally have a shot of vodka in the morning to steady my nerves before going to work. However, I am successful and in time I am promoted to P6000 Technical Specialist. Then my luck runs out.

One Tuesday evening, I decide to go to the Affair nightclub alone. I have abandoned my aging mini and now drive an old brown Ford Cortina. I arrive at the club at around 9pm and have several pints of lager. I chat to a few people I know and then look for girls. Towards the end of the evening I drink two pints of water to help clear my head. It's a normal night out and I feel fine. Then I meet an old pal from school.

"Let me get you a beer," says Dave.

"No, better not - I'm leaving soon."

"Oh come on. For old time's sake. One beer won't hurt."

"OK, I'll have a lager." I don't really want it but he's an old friend. One beer won't hurt.

I see the large white police van in my rear view mirror. I am heading home down East Hill and one glance at my speedometer tells me what I don't want to know. I am speeding. It's late, the streets are quiet and I am very, very sure that the policeman in the van has got nothing better to do than check me out.

The traffic lights at the bottom of East Hill turn from green to amber. If I hit the hammer down, I could just beat the red light and the police van might have to stop. Fortunately, I am not that drunk or that stupid. I stop at the red light. When the lights turn green again, I play 'I am a very careful driver' as I cautiously drive towards my parents house. The police van follows. On the outskirts of the town, the siren wails and the blue lights flash and I pull over. I get a sense of déjà vu as I discuss speeding, drinking and breathalysers with the police officer. I fail the new electronic breath test. Next on the agenda is the blood test at the nick.

A doctor is summoned, probably from his bed, and a sample of my blood is taken. Then, after a few hours in an office and another breath test (negative this time), I am released into the cold morning air. I wasn't even held in the cells.

Several weeks later I receive an official looking letter from the Magistrates Court. It's my court date. The blood test is over the limit but a quick check of the figures shows it was close. You are given a 10% margin for error but I am 13% over. I am unlucky. About time too.

In court I wear a shirt and tie and a smart -v-necked pullover. I don't want to wear a suit and give the impression I am an armed robber. The three magistrates seem friendly and one asks if I have a lawyer. I don't.

"Do you want one?" he asks.

"No thank you, your honour." Just get it over with. They are not going to shoot me. Drink driving is serious but it is not the capital offence that it is today.

In my defence I state the bleeding obvious; I am sorry; I wasn't that much over the limit; I have no previous driving convictions. (The last one is true so laugh all you want.) I am given a £130 fine and a years driving ban.

"How do you want to pay?" the court secretary asks.

I consider replying "American Express" to see if the secretary will respond "That'll do nicely," but instead write a cheque and get the bus home.

Chapter 9: Brothel Diversions

After 5 years working on the P6000, I am getting a bit bored and I am casting about looking for a new job using Unix.

After I lost my driving licence, I bought a house on the Fernlea estate off Bergholt Road so that I could walk to work. I got the license back after a year but now that I live in town, I can party and then get a taxi home. No more drink/driving. At least that's the theory.

One day my current boss, who is a great guy called Joe, calls me into his office and says he's heard that I might be looking for a new challenge. He explains that there is another range of Philips' computers called the P7000 and the support team in Marlow (West London) is being restructured. There is an opening for a new UK support person to help with the migration to Unix. It would mean a company car, mobile phone plus training, more responsibility and independence.

"How do you fancy it?" Joe asks.

"Company car? Where do I sign?" I reply.

Restructuring. Fucking restructuring. If you ever hear these words run a fucking mile. I get my company car and drive the two and a half hours around the M25 motorway to Marlow to meet the guy who'll show me the ropes on the P7000 range of computers. His name is Graham and he's a salesman (or account executive) but he used to be a trainer so he's a bit more technical than your average salesman.

"Are you any good?" he asks after we have introduced ourselves.

"Yes I think so; I am one of the best technical specialists at Elektra House."

"Well I hope so because they've sacked everyone technical at this office except me. That means it's you and me to look after over 100 customers all over the UK."

"Why did they sack everyone?" I ask.

"Some sort of office politics. The bosses here and at Elektra couldn't get on so Elektra booted the Marlow guys out."

Joe hadn't told me about this.
"Got a company car?" Graham asks.
I nod.
"Good, you'll need it - it's gonna be fucking chaos."

I spend a week with Graham at Marlow. I read everything - technical reports, bug fixes, known patches, manuals. Fortunately the documentation is good and the development systems have been well maintained. This is (was) a good team they have fired - I am impressed but also very worried.

It is virtually impossible to take on a completely new mini computer system when you have an installed user base of 100 customers and zero training. Graham is good and I work very, very hard. The hardware guys supporting this system are also excellent. Maybe, just maybe, this impossible job can be made to work.

Finally I get a weeks training in Apeldoorn, Holland, where the European support centre for Philips is based. This helps a lot and now at least I can get telephone support from a bunch of Dutch guys who know this system inside out.

The weeks turn to months and years. I drive the length and breadth of the country meeting the customers, fixing problems and doing upgrades. I live in hotels, eat on expenses and drink heavily. Graham likes his beer too and we get on well together socially and with customers. He's a big guy full of largesse and salesmanship. I am his technical wizard. He sells, I deliver. However, there is a problem. The migration of this proprietary system to the Unix environment is not going well. In fact what is supposed to be an automatic process just doesn't work. Also the technology has moved on and Windows has appeared in the market as a serious competitor to small mini-computer systems.

At this time Graham and I are joined by another P7000 wizard who has been working at a big P7000 installation at a Philips' factory in Blackburn. His name is Mike and he makes my drinking habits of the time look like small beer. Mike and I decide to go to Apeldoorn to get a complete briefing on the Unix migration problems and to see if we can help. We also intend to get very drunk and to get laid if at all possible - Mike has been reliably informed of the name of a brothel in the town and we're going to try and find it.

We arrive at our Tulip Hotel in Apeldoorn late in the afternoon. Our meeting with the Dutch team is tomorrow morning. This gives us all night to explore the seamier side of life. Mike is older than me - late thirties probably - but he is heavily-bearded and world weary looking so it is hard to tell his age. He is married with one small child but still likes to play the field if given the chance. After a shower, we meet in the hotel bar about six in the evening.

"Two large Southern Comforts, on the rocks," Mike tells the barman. It has become a tradition for Mike and I to begin a drinking session with large Southern Comforts.

Together with Graham, we support over 100 customers paying software license fees totalling nearly one million pounds a year. Hardware support is extra. There are only three of us, we cost virtually nothing and we are doing the job previously done by 7 or 8 people. We are a very profitable team and we can do pretty much as we like so long as our customers are happy. And after several years hard work by the three of us, our customers are happy - except with the Unix migration.

Several Southern Comforts later, Mike and I venture into town. We eat at a steak house and then visit a bar, where we find Dutch girls are quite interested in a pair of outrageously intoxicated English computer experts with a ribald sense of polite conversation. We ask two girls where we can find our brothel. They giggle and ask us how much we are prepared to pay. Unfortunately we need a receipt (for expenses purposes) so we decline their suggestive offer and make our way to the taxi rank.

Life tip: If you are ever in a strange town and want to know where the brothels are - go to the taxi rank.

We hop in a taxi and Mike tells the driver the name of our brothel. In a few minutes we are delivered to a large, heavy wooden door with what looks like a peep hole facing the street. It's a normal looking residential area. I ring the buzzer and, after a prolonged pause, the door is opened by an aging woman wearing a negligee who escorts us inside and asks us where we are from and how we are doing tonight. She ushers us into a large bar area on the ground floor of the house where there is a small stage and a few tables and chairs. Seated at one table is a man who is talking to and caressing a scantily clad girl. There are several bored-looking girls sitting by the stage. Let's be totally honest about this; Mike and I are both drunk but years of drinking mean that we can function like this and appear relatively normal. We sit at the bar, order Southern Comforts and wonder what to do next. We glance over at the girls but it is quite dark and hard to tell which ones might be good looking at this distance. We make small talk with our aging hostess who, on realising our inexperience in this process, prompts two of the girls to approach us. My one is pretty enough, with dark hair and tanned skin, but a bit plump. Mike's is thinner, almost skinny, with slightly afro hair and bad teeth. He seems happy with her. We buy them drinks and negotiate a price. Mike hands over his credit card, which is kept behind the bar.

Upstairs my girl takes me into a bedroom, undresses me and then takes off her bra and panties. I ask her about her life - it is a sad story. She plays with my dick. Somehow she gets a condom on my flaccid weapon and begins sucking. My heart isn't in it. I feel sad and empty. I feel sorry for her and stroke her gently. She gives up sucking.

After a while we go downstairs and I buy her another drink. Mike and his girl appear a short time later and we buy more drinks and order a taxi. When the taxi arrives, we pay our bill and get a receipt. 'Diversions' is apparently what we did upstairs. I think it's Dutch for sundries. As we leave I think I see a copulating couple in the corner of the bar. A man seems to be sitting in a chair with his trousers down while a girl, facing and astride him, bobs up and down. Maybe it's a trick of the light. The door closes behind us and the world of sundries is over. Until the next time.

"Yeah - I fucked her good," Mike exclaims once we are safely in our taxi.

"Yeah, me too. Fucking brilliant," I concur. Actually I have just realised that I am bursting for a piss but we'll soon be at our hotel - I hope.

At the hotel I get my room key and hurry to the lift. Room 455; fourth floor, right? Wrong. I explore the entire floor and can't find my room. I am very drunk and desperate to pee. I explore further but, overcome by a full bladder, and by now completely lost in the large hotel complex, I find myself unzipping my fly on some well-polished wooden backstairs and pissing down them in a never ending waterfall, which cascades onwards and downwards to I know not where.

I am later found wandering in a hotel kitchen by a night porter who escorts me to my room - number 455 on the second floor extension.

The meeting with the Dutch does not go well. They buy us lunch in an expensive restaurant and I have to fight hard not to throw up in front of everyone. The wine with the meal helps calm my nerves and ease my hangover. Mike is feeling slightly better than me so I let him do the talking; I just nod appropriately and try not to puke.

The Dutch tell us of problems. The migration to Unix will not be automatic. It will be a manual process carried out by the team in Holland and it will be done on a time-and-materials basis for each customer who wants it. It's bad news - the manual process will be very expensive. No one will pay this much for Old World technology. This gravy train has come to a grinding halt. I finish the wine - it might be the last free wine for a while.

Chapter 10: Car Wars

I am in Scotland doing a P7000 software upgrade. I drove the five hundred miles to Scotland yesterday and stayed overnight in a comfortable hotel. The upgrade is a major one and quite time consuming. I start early in the morning and it is lunch time before I am finished. I spend the afternoon running tests and making a few minor configuration changes.

I am planning to spend tonight in the same hotel I stayed in last night so that I can rest after my long drive yesterday. On the way back to the hotel I get a phone call. It's Graham.

"We've got an urgent problem with the Mitcham site in London. Can you go there tomorrow? I'd send Mike but he's off sick."

"But I'm in Scotland," I wail.

"Couldn't you drive down tonight? Please."

"OK." I really don't want to drive back home tonight. I am very tired. At the hotel I check out. Then I drive towards the motorway and settle in for the long ride south. I like driving and I am happy to drive for hours without stopping, listening to heavy metal or rock music. I should be home before midnight.

By 9pm I have made very good time and I am less than two hours from home. I have left the motorway and am now heading cross country looking for somewhere to eat. At the very least I deserve a meal on expenses for this effort. On the edge of Cambridge there is an Indian restaurant I often eat at when I am driving this route. In the restaurant I order a curry and a bottle of wine. My nerves are jangling from the long drive and I need some alcohol.

The meal is finished, the wine bottle is empty and I am feeling relaxed. It's 10pm and I am getting sleepy. But there are only two hours to go and I know all the short cuts home from here. I drive fast. It helps to keep me awake. There is very little traffic about and I am only fifteen minutes from home.

Do I nod off? I don't know. Do I hit the kerb? I don't know. Does my tyre blow out? I don't know. Suddenly the car is out of control. I try to correct the skid but fail and I career across the road not far in front of an oncoming car. I miss a telephone pole by a few yards. The car mounts the pavement on the other side of the road, leaps a ditch and buries itself in a corn field. I am unscathed.

I get out of the car breathing heavily and walk back to the road. The car I nearly hit head-on has stopped. The driver opens his passenger door and leans over.

"Are you OK?" he calls out. He seems very calm despite the fact that I nearly killed him.

"Yeah," I say, walking up to the open car door.

"Do you want a cigarette?" He offers me one. I sit in the empty passenger seat and smoke the cigarette.

"Have you been drinking?" he says with a laugh. This guy's as crazy as me.

"I had a couple of beers," I say. The car driver laughs again.

"Do you want a lift somewhere?" he asks.

"No it's OK, I'll call for a taxi," I say. "There's a pub a few hundred yards back."

He drives me to the pub.

"Take care mate. You're a lucky bastard," he says as he drives off.

I think he was lucky too. If we had hit head-on either God would have had two more angels or more likely Satan would have had two more souls to fry.

Life tip: Alcohol and driving don't mix.

Life tip: Tiredness and driving don't mix.

(Yes, I know you know this but then so did I.)

At the pub I ring for a cab and in half an hour I am home. It's a little after midnight. I ring an all night vehicle recovery firm. I explain where the car is and go to bed. At 1am the phone rings.

"Hello, Sir. Vehicle recovery here, Sir. I can't find your car."

"Well you better come and pick me up and I'll show you where it is."

I dress and am shortly picked up in a huge tow truck. We drive to the scene of the accident. The tow truck driver shines a very bright light in the direction I indicate. It's no wonder he couldn't find the car, it is a good fifteen yards into the corn field. The tow truck driver smiles.

"That's some accident," he says.

Yeah tell me about it, I think to myself. The car is winched aboard the tow truck and by 4am I am asleep in my bed.

I get four hours sleep and then go to work. I explain to my manager Joe that I have had an accident and I need to hire a car.

"No problem," says Joe. "You are all right are you?"

"Yeah fine."

"How's the car?" he asks.

"A write-off."

"Really? That must have been some accident."

In my hire car I drive to Mitcham. I fix their problem. Everyone is happy. I am extremely tired. I drive home slowly and sleep. I sleep for a very, very long time.

Chapter 11: Farewell to Bachelorhood

Gradually customers drift away from the P7000. Mike leaves to do some sort of Unix job at Amdahl and Graham gets reposted within Philips to a division that is still selling something. I am on my own. I get training in Unix and start playing with Windows. There are a few Unix customers for Philips but they do not use the migration software and are mostly located in the north of the country. They are supported out of the Prestwich office (near Manchester). I don't have much to do. I have taken to taking a hip flask full of vodka to work to keep me going between liquid pub lunches at the Bricklayers Arms. I am looking into a black hole of depression. My skills are out of date. My debts are high. My love life has come to a complete standstill. I am drinking way too much.

Then, early one Monday morning, I get a phone call from Tan Choudry. He's the Marketing Manager on the new range of Unix boxes Philips are badge-engineering from Motorola and he wants to talk. In his office, I wonder what the hell he wants. I've never met him before.

"Paul, we're making a big push with these new Unix boxes. I need a Product Manager. I've been told that you're the man for the job. What do you say?"

Fuck me. I wasn't expecting this. Tan continues.

"Of course, there'd be a promotion, pension benefits, the usual manager's perks, upgraded company car, etc. How about it?"

"How does 'yes' sound." I only need to be asked twice. We shake hands. I am a manager. Just like that. A manager with a hip flask full of vodka in my pocket and absolutely no idea what a product manager does. Ooops.

I get a bit of training: presentation skills, time management, chairing a meeting, problem solving, decision making and all that kind of managerial stuff. My basic responsibility is to get the product 'released'. Released means that the salesmen can sell it. Once Holland releases some new product the UK can also release it. This happens after I've written a report on it and got all the engineering and software managers to sign it off. It's a nightmare. No one wants to sign stuff off because once it's signed off they have to support it. And there's so many new products; Oracle databases, word processors, spreadsheets, SCSI drives, tape drives. A cornucopia of new software and hardware every month. And every customer wants something different and new releases and upgrades. It's never ending. But it's a job. And the new Marketing Executive, Mark, is a good guy. Likes a drink. Likes a laugh. Life could be worse.

Mark has finally decided to do it and a date has been set. All that is required now is an appropriate farewell to bachelorhood. Mark's best man, Andrew, has organised a stag do to Amsterdam. There are five of us going; Mark, myself, Andrew and two of Mark and Andrew's old friends, John and Keith.

Andrew, John and Keith are driving down from Manchester, where Mark is originally from, and we will meet them on the Friday night ferry from Felixstowe. Mark and I are getting a lift to Felixstowe from his wife-to-be, Cathy. We plan to party all weekend.

At Felixstowe Mark says his farewell to his beloved and we hurry onboard the ferry and make for the bar. We find Andrew, John and Keith are already seated at a table drinking. The overnight crossing is nine hours and we will arrive in the Hague in the very early morning. Then it's a short train ride to Amsterdam.

We spend several hours drinking before bedding down anywhere that looks reasonably comfortable. We have not booked cabins as this is intended to be a budget holiday. Andrew, John and Keith appear to have very little money - I am not sure that they are gainfully employed in Manchester.

We arrive in the Hague a little the worse for wear and in need of a shower, a change of clothes and a stiff drink. However, before we can find any of these we must get the train to Amsterdam. On the train we buy lager.

Amsterdam is packed with tourists. The good hotels are full, the budget hotels are full, and the youth hostels are full. Eventually, Andrew, John and Keith find a room they can share in a hostel. It has communal toilets and showers and is very, very basic. Mark and I arrange to meet the others later and go and look for something more palatial. We find a room in a one star hotel but it does have a private toilet and shower. We can only stay one night, however, so tomorrow we shall have to find something else.

After a shower, we stow our gear in the room and venture out into the warm, sunny afternoon and begin to look for our companions. We find them as expected in a cannabis café in the red light area. They are giggling uncontrollably and completely stoned. They can't even hold a conversation. Mark decides to join them and orders a joint. I tell him that I'm going to explore and I'll find him later.

Beautiful women fascinate me. They always have, they always will. It's my Achilles heel. I'll do almost anything to be in the company of beautiful women. To hold them, to touch them, to love them, to fuck them. I'll do anything - I'll even pay (within reason of course).

Wandering the red light area is interesting. It's prostitution at its most efficient. The deal can be done and the transaction executed in less than twenty minutes. I wander into a bar and order a whisky and lemonade. A petite Asian girl wanders over to me.

"Hello. I'm Rachel. Are you looking for company?"

"Well, I'll buy you a drink if you like."

"That would be nice," she says. She orders a gin and tonic while I study her. She is a light chocolate colour with perfect white teeth and very long, straight black hair. She must be about 22 or 23. Her eyes are bright and clear and she doesn't appear to be high.

"Would you like to come next door?" she says. "I have a room. Only 100 guilders for as long as you want."

She is wearing a short blue top showing her flat midriff and white tight-fitting slacks. Her breasts are small but then that's what I like.

"OK. Let's have one more drink and then go next door," I say.

As we drink I caress her and she fondles my groin. She tells me that she's working to make money which she sends to her family in the Philippines. The money pays for her little brother to go to school.

She takes me to a room across the narrow street. It's small and functional with just a bed and a basin. She's enthusiastic and keen to please. I am as horny as hell. She removes her top and her white slacks, climbs onto the edge of the bed, sticks her arse in the air and lays with her head on a pillow.

"Take my panties off and fuck me dog style. I like it best that way," she says.

I like it that way too, I think to myself as I prepare to do the deed.

After my exertions, I go drinking until quite late. When my head begins to swim, I decide its time to head back to the hotel. On my way I pass the bar where I met my Asian whore. Just by chance I see her crossing the road to her room of business. She is leading by the hand an extremely fat, bearded fellow who is obviously very drunk. I wonder whether he will get the same delightful service that I received. I hope not.

At the hotel, I sleep fitfully. Mark crashes in at about 3am. He is as high as a kite but eventually he settles into his bed.

In the morning we rise late and both of us have bad headaches. Swallowing painkillers we pack our things - we have to find a new hotel room for tonight. Mark tells me about his cannabis night. I tell him about my Asian. I think he is jealous, but then he is getting married.

Staggering outside into the bright sunshine, we make for the tourist office near the main railway station to see if they know of any available hotel rooms. The streets are packed with people and the nearer to the train station we get, the more crowded it becomes. The queue at the tourist office is enormous. Mark is discouraged.

"Maybe we should just go home," he says. I think he feels tired and sick. I try to stay optimistic.

"Let's just try one or two more hotels back in the centre," I say.

"OK," he agrees.

We begin walking back to the city centre, carrying our bags, when a young man on a bicycle shouts to us.

"Are you looking for a room?"

I nod yes and he comes over.

"Hello. My name's Andre. Are you looking for a room?" he asks again.

Mark is hesitant.

"Yes," I say. "A room for two for tonight."

"Well, I have an apartment with rooms for hire," says Andre.

"How much?" I ask.

"I have a twin room for 200 guilders. It's not far."

Mark doesn't trust the guy. I say we might as well look at it.

After a five minute walk we are at the apartment in the city centre. The room is fine with a toilet, shower and two single beds. Mark is still unsure.

"Look Mark, it's either this or we go home. What have we got to lose?"

"OK. We'll take it," he says.

We hand over the money and Andre gives us a set of keys to the front door.

"We'll be leaving early in the morning," I tell him.

"Please put the keys through the letter box when you leave," says Andre as he leaves us to sell his one remaining room for hire. Who is the more trusting I wonder - us or Andre? Mark decides to sleep so I leave the apartment to explore.

I return a couple of hours later to find Mark wide awake and dressed.

"I woke up and found Andre in our room," he says.

"What did he say?" I ask.

"He said he was looking for something he'd lost."

"Well he's probably as nervous of us as we are of him. Just relax. It's not like we've got much worth nicking."

"I suppose." Mark finally relaxes and we get ready for the evening's action.

We find Andrew, John and Keith in a bar in the red light district. They are drinking but are still relatively sober as it is still early. The five of us wander from bar to bar drinking heavily and behaving badly. In one bar I need to puke and retire to the toilet to find it is just a hole in the ground surrounded by tiles (these are quite common in Holland). I bend over the hole and throw up. I feel better. Too much beer disagrees with me. I switch to spirits.

The others seem set to drink all night. Me? I want to get laid. I bid the others farewell and fight my way through the crowded bar to the street outside. Everywhere is crowded. I skirt the edge of the red light district where it is quieter and the girls seem more eager for business. A big-chested black girl taps on her glass window and beckons me over.

"You want good fuck and suck?" She smiles broadly. "I'll show you a good time." She quickly removes her white bra and shows me her gravity-defying breasts. Then she turns around and shakes her full-some backside provocatively in a way only black women seem able to do.

I enter her small glass-fronted room. I fuck her doggy style. Then I flip her over, remove the condom and masturbate until I spray spunk over her large firm breasts. She is giggling as the spunk runs down her tits and drips off the end of her nipples.

"You're gorgeous," I tell her. I mean it.

"Thank you, Sir," she says.

If only I was staying another night. I would definitely see her again.

I find Mark and the others in a bar - they are completely smashed. I order large whiskies and am soon smashed too. On our way home, Mark and I buy pizza before crashing out in our room. The alarm wakes us early and in a haze we pack and make for the train station. The train ride and the ferry home are an alcoholic blur as we swallow lager by the crate.

Arriving in Felixstowe, Andrew, John and Keith find their car and begin the long drive north. Mark and I are met by Cathy. It's been a stag do that I will not quickly forget.

Chapter 12: Cue Prologue

At the Bricklayers Arms there's a new barmaid. Jenny's young (19), pretty and has a cute arse. Mark and I have been admiring her for the last couple of days during our lunch time drinking sessions. Mark is now safely married so his interest is largely academic.

"How's your boyfriend?" I ask her as she is drying glasses.

"Oh, we just broke up. He is seeing another girl. Got her pregnant."

"Well, do you fancy a night out with me?" I am much too old for her (I am 28) but if you don't ask you don't get.

"Yeah OK - what about tonight?"

I am obviously on a roll. This girl is really cute. One quarter Japanese, petite and slightly Asian looking. And she seems to move fast - I like that.

I pick her up at her parents' house in my new manager's company car. Nothing special; blue 2 litre Cavalier with a CD player and sun-roof. Not spectacular but brand new. Her parents seem to like me. I am a young looking 28 (despite my drinking) and could probably pass for 25. I am smart but casual, clean shaven and friendly. A wolf in sheep's clothing? No, more of a pussy cat.

We go to a quiet pub to talk, then out clubbing. I keep my drinking under control and deliver her home safe and sound in the early hours. We kiss and cuddle. I like this girl.

"Will you see me again?" I whisper.

"Yes please," she says.

It's the start of a five year relationship.

Work is tough. Philips isn't aggressive enough in its adoption of Unix and got into the market too late. The computer division is haemorrhaging millions. Holland doesn't release new products quickly enough and the bureaucracy is stifling. I am releasing as much new product as anyone in the marketing group but it is obvious that the writing is on the wall. There is a rumour that Philips will buy Olivetti but in the end the deal falls through and everyone is waiting for the inevitable redundancies.

The bright spot in my life is Jenny. Her youth and vitality rejuvenate me. I reduce my alcohol consumption. We fuck like rabbits.

"Do you want to move in with me?" I ask her one Friday night after an especially satisfactory bedroom session.

"How about tomorrow?" she says.

"Tomorrow it is."

Saturday arrives and I drive over to pick her up with her stuff. It's a tryout, I tell myself. We'll live together to see if it works. If it doesn't we'll just part as friends and move on. Well, that's the plan.

Jenny had gone home early to pack a 'few things' and I arrive to have lunch with her parents and bring her back permanently. After lunch Jenny shows me what she has packed. It's everything. Everything she owns in the world. I am reminded of my drive to university with my mini full of all my belongings. She has committed to me - completely. I am moved by her sense of trust but I am frightened that I am not worthy of it.

Living together works out. She is everything I want. Beautiful, funny, good in bed, good company. I am in love again. In the evenings we eat the food she has cooked for us, watch television, giggle, laugh and I drink. Later in bed we talk, make love and make plans for the future.

What future? Philips is going bust. It's just a matter of time. Everyone is hanging on for the redundancy money. I start drinking hard again and almost continuously. Vodka at breakfast, hip flask, liquid lunch, hip flask, evening of whisky. It's well over a bottle of spirits a day but I am still functioning. Just.

Finally the phone at my desk rings. It's the senior marketing manager, John Williams. He used to be Tan's boss but Tan has already jumped ship. Walking to John's office I know what to expect. The rumour mill has been working overtime. Digital Equipment Corporation (DEC) have agreed to buy all of Philips Computer Division in Europe for one billion dollars. (DEC subsequently got into trouble themselves and were bought by Compaq, who have just been bought by Hewlett Packard. Things move fast in the computer industry.) There are to be many layoffs. There is widespread duplication of functions so downsizing is inevitable.

"Paul, I have some bad news," John begins. I leave his office without my company car keys and carrying a large brown envelope containing amongst other things a cheque for £16,263.

Cue prologue.

Chapter 13: Interview Hell

Things are pretty desperate. I don't think I am employable with the drink problem. I've spent much of the sixteen thousand pounds clearing credit card debts and paying the mortgage. I also feel completely responsible for Jenny, who is supportive but doesn't realise the amount I am drinking or the hole I am in.

All my recent experience is as a Product Manager but I don't really enjoy this work. Product Management is technical but it is also marketing - it requires higher levels of sociability than I naturally possess. I'd really like to go back to programming and working more closely with computers. However, it is now two years since I did any real programming work and my skills are now two years out of date.

My Product Manager's CV looks good. All those made redundant by Philips were put up in a hotel for a week and a bunch of recruitment consultants gave us career advice and help with CV preparation. It looks as if I'm doomed to spend the rest of my life in marketing. I scan the relevant job pages in the computer press. A recruitment agency is advertising for a Unix Product Manager. It's a good fit with my old Philips' job so I give the agency a call and send in my CV. They are very interested and want to interview me immediately. Their client is a big computer manufacturer. It's a prestigious company, a prestigious job and a prestigious salary.

An interview is arranged at the agent's offices in North West London for the Monday afternoon of the following week. I work out the timings and find that I need to leave Colchester fairly early in the morning to get the train to London. Then it's a longish tube ride followed by a taxi to their office. The interview is at 2pm. Everything is in place except for one thing - my calculation is that my hip flask won't hold enough vodka to keep me calm for the whole journey. I decide to take a half bottle of vodka in my overcoat pocket just to be sure that I have enough alcohol to stave off the shakes.

The trip begins well enough. My skin has deteriorated due to the alcohol abuse of the last few years and I have now grown a short beard so that I don't have to shave. But I am well turned out in my newly pressed suit and well-polished shoes. I have a few nips of the neat vodka on the train. I am not planning to drink the whole bottle before the interview - I will just drink what I need. I will then throw away what is left in the bottle before I reach the agent's offices. My overriding priority is to be calm - interviews are bad enough without symptoms of alcohol withdrawal creating more panic.

I have had very few interviews during my ten years at Philips but we did practice them on the redundancy course and I am hopeful of giving a good performance. I should arrive in plenty of time feeling relaxed and calm, having drunk the absolute minimum of alcohol to keep me functioning.

Then disaster strikes - the train is held up between Chelmsford and London for over half an hour. The power lines are down or there are leaves on the line or something. I don't own a mobile phone so I can't ring the agent. I can probably still make the interview on time but my stress level is rising. So is my vodka intake.

In London, I hurry for the tube. My pulse is racing and I am beginning to sweat. More nips of vodka. I am drinking more than I estimated I would need. On the tube ride I am constantly looking at my watch and hoping the underground train will go faster. Finally we are at my stop. It's 1-30pm. I could still just make the appointment if only I can find a taxi quickly. I hail one with its yellow 'Taxi' light glowing brightly indicating that it's available for hire.

I climb aboard and give the driver the address. The driver doesn't know this area well and we make several wrong turns. He gets out his A to Z. I notice that I have now nearly finished the half bottle of vodka and am feeling a little bit woozy. Suddenly I see the agent's office but the driver can't get to it because of the one-way system. The vodka bottle is empty. I get out of the taxi, pay the driver and run for the office. I am twenty minutes late. As I run I look for a bin where I can throw the empty bottle of vodka. I can't find one. I give up looking and put the empty bottle back into my overcoat pocket.

In the office I meet the agent and smile. He takes my overcoat and hangs it on a coat-stand in reception. He leads me into a meeting room with a circular table. He begins his questions and I give appropriate responses. Things are going well but I must smell of alcohol. My performance is reasonable - he is non-committal but friendly. He says that they'll get back to me. I try to look interested and keen.

Back in reception he pulls my overcoat from the coat-stand but as he does so he fumbles and drops it. The empty bottle of vodka bounces out of its hiding place in the coat's pocket and into full view. I retrieve both items, look at him and shrug. It is now obvious that I have just drunk half a bottle of vodka. As I leave he shakes my hand but they never get in touch. Who would blame them?

Chapter 14: Eroticism on Legs

I decide to give up Marketing and Product Management. I am just not suited to it and it is very boring. The only other skill I can really sell is my knowledge of the P7000/Unix migration software, which I understand reasonably well but it is not much in demand in the UK. I decide to call a Dutch contracting agency. I am in luck.

"Do you know anything about the P7000/Unix migration software?" the agent asks after I explain my situation. I can't believe my ears.

"Yes, yes (yes!) that's what I have been working on for the last two years." This is a lie - for the last two years I've been a product manager writing technical reports but I have got all the manuals and I can read. The agent sets up a telephone interview with his client for early Monday morning. I have the weekend to read manuals.

Monday morning arrives. I've been reading all weekend with virtually no sleep. At the prearranged time the phone rings. After some preliminaries, Adolf says he would like to ask me some technical questions. Fortunately his English is not good so he will probably keep it short. He just wants a warm body. Anybody. I have all the manuals in front of me and tensely await the interrogation. The first two questions are straightforward and I can answer them. Then he asks me if I can give some examples of symbolic references I have used in the migration software. Fuck. Symbolic references. I vaguely remember reading something. I stall for time and begin rifling through the manuals. Time passes - it's becoming embarrassing. Suddenly I find the page I have been looking for entitled 'Symbolic References'. Thank God. I read some out and I sound convincing - I am, after all, a technical specialist. He's convinced. I'm in. Hilversum, Holland here we come.

I talk to the agent again. The contract is for six months and accommodation will be provided. I will be paid twenty five pounds an hour - that's a thousand pounds a week. I begin packing but then a problem materialises - no partners can be accommodated. Jenny will have to stay home. She's gutted and I'm annoyed but I need the money - we both know it. I tell her that she can come over in a few weeks and find an apartment for both of us.

I fly to Schipol airport in Amsterdam and the agent meets me and drives me to Hilversum. I have been drinking on the plane but I am not expected to work today. Arriving at the company accommodation, I am introduced to the other three male inmates. They are all young men, eager but hardly tested in the fire of development. At 31 I feel old, very old. There are two Dutch guys and one Irishman. I spend the evening talking to the Irishman and drinking from a bottle of whisky I have brought from England. I will not be working with these guys, they are on other projects. They are just house-mates. I wish Jenny was here.

The next day I am taken to work by one of the Dutch guys who is working at the same huge A.T.&T. factory as myself. He shows me to reception and then disappears into the maze of corridors to find his own project, his own work-mates. I had a little port this morning (it was all I could find in the local shop) but I am feeling reasonably fresh. I meet Adolf and his team. They are all younger than me and very confident. We have a meeting and they explain their system to me. It is very, very complicated. Probably too complicated. I begin work and at lunch time I read manuals. I will read manuals every lunch time for the next few weeks. I read manuals in a bar, drinking whisky.

After two weeks of this I am going slowly mad. I don't get on with my house-mates and drinking in bars alone in the evenings is depressing. I don't speak Dutch so I can't mix with the locals. The system we are writing is too complex and will probably never work. I don't tell anyone this, obviously.

One Friday evening after several large whiskies I do the predictable: I go to the taxi rank.

"Can you take me somewhere they have girls?" I say.

"Ah, you want girls." The taxi driver nods knowingly and sets off.

A few minutes later I am at the door of a respectable residential address. I ring the bell and feel almost like an old hand. The routine is familiar. I plant myself at the bar next to a gorgeous looking black girl wearing a tight bikini. I introduce myself. She is really lovely with dark chocolate skin, a fantastic figure and a beautiful smile. She's fun to talk to and I buy her drinks of Piccolo champagne. It tastes like watered down piss but then it probably is.

Her name is Monica. She is a 23 year old illegal immigrant trying to earn enough money to buy a marriage.

"Are you married?" she asks.

"No," I reply.

"I'll pay you 3000 dollars to marry me," she says.

She's serious and, with all the whisky in me, I am tempted. She is eroticism on legs. She looks like a great fuck. I hand over my gold American Express card and we go upstairs.

Monica looks even better naked with her shaven pussy and large firm breasts. My dick is as stiff as a board and she slides the condom on easily. As I lie stretched out on my back, she sucks greedily on my dick before moving herself up and sliding my erect member into her warm, wet cunt. With her feet flat on the bed, she rides me for a while, bobbing up and down, moaning and licking her lips. It's a good show. Then she stands up and towering over me says "I like you - I'll give you something special." She reaches down, slips the condom off and proceeds to give me the best blow job of my life. It's ecstasy. I'm just about to come when she says "Now fuck me. Fuck me hard." She rolls onto her back next to me and spreads her legs as wide as possible. In an instant I am banging away at her juicy pussy.

"Oh I like you. Fuck me. Fuck me," she begs. As she moans, I climax. It feels beautiful. A complete release. Immediately I've come, she's licking and sucking on my dick again. I am in love. This is the best fuck of my life. Ever.

There's a knock at the door and the brothel madam tells me that my two hours is up and do I want another two hours. Yes, I say. I end up staying all night, which costs me six hundred pounds but it is worth every penny.

In the very early morning, waiting for my taxi, I slip Monica my address on a piece of paper. It's Saturday today and all the other guys go back to their real homes for the weekend so I have the house to myself.

"I'll come and see you later at 4pm," she whispers. I don't believe her.

Back at home, I sleep. I wake up again around 3pm and have a shower. I drink some more port. She won't come. At 4 o'clock, standing in my bathrobe, I glance out of the window. A beautiful, statuesque black girl is walking towards the house. It's Monica. She is wearing a light, breezy trouser suit and I can feel a stiffening in my loins. I let her in. She looks ravishing. I look a wreck.

I take her to my room where she immediately notices the hard-on under the bathrobe.

"Do you want to fuck me now and then I thought we'd go to Amsterdam."

It's not really a question; it's a command. Pulling off the trousers of her trouser suit, I fuck her doggy style on the carpet while she purrs happily.

"Get dressed while I have a quick shower," she says.

"Yes ma'am," I reply.

We take the train to Amsterdam and have a romantic Chinese meal. I do like Monica. She's witty, funny, clever and just the best fuck ever. I consider proposing marriage. Back at Hilversum station, I kiss her as we say goodbye.

"I'll come and see you next Friday," I promise. I never do. Monica did give me something special. The clap.

Chapter 15: Politie

I get my clap sorted out and Jenny comes over and finds us a big holiday caravan to rent together. I cycle to work and my parents come for a visit. The end of the contract is in sight. It's been hell really and I don't think the system will ever work properly. Fortunately, by the time they start full system testing, I will be long gone. Their decision, not mine.

There's a bit of money in the bank now but it won't last long back in England. Another worry won't leave my mind. Aids. Look, let's face it; I fucked a whore without protection and got the clap. A nice whore, I liked her. But maybe I've got HIV, maybe I've given it to Jenny. I can't get it out of my mind.

Back in England I go to the local VD clinic for a test. They couldn't test me in Holland because it takes six months for the HIV antibodies to show up. It's now been six months since I fucked the beautiful Monica. The day of reckoning is upon me.

The doctor calls me into her office.

"You know how dangerous unprotected sex is don't you?" she begins.

Look, I've got a fucking degree in Biology, bitch, I know everything.

"Yes, I have been foolish," I say.

"Well, you're very lucky and you're test is negative, this time."

"Thanks very much." I try hard not to smile. OK. Panic over. Now I need a job.

Back at home with Jenny, I get an unexpected phone call.

"Hi, is that Paul?" a voice asks.

"Yes, speaking."

"Well, this is Phil Williams of Imasys in Manchester and I've got a proposition for you." It turns out that a small part of the old UK Philips P6000 business wasn't sold to DEC but was subject to a management buy-out. The new company formed in the process is called Imasys and it is based in Manchester. They need somebody for about a year to upgrade the software of all their P6000 customers - about sixty in all. It's a long time since I worked on P6000 but I need the work and the money. We make a deal. One years contract for thirty thousand pounds plus expenses. Not exactly £25 an hour but it's a buyers market and I'm desperate.

I drive to Manchester and check into the Piccadilly hotel. I live there for around a month until I find somewhere to rent within walking distance of the office. Jenny joins me and we rent out the house in Colchester.

After a year, the contract is complete but Phil has a new offer. Stay in Manchester and work on their new system as permanent staff earning 23K a year. It's a steal. Imasys are fucking me up the arse but they know 3 things:

1) I am old and my skill set is well past its sell by date.
2) I am an alcoholic.
3) 1 & 2 make me virtually unemployable anywhere else.

What is the definition of an alcoholic? My definition is that a user becomes an addict once the body's metabolism has become dependent on the drug. In other words you need the drug to feel normal. Nothing to do with being drunk. If you don't have your drug you become ill. Of course, if you do have your drug you become ill, just more slowly.

I begin work on the 'new' system which is written in Microfocus Cobol. It's already old technology! The system's a dog. Badly written, unreliable, difficult to maintain. This system will haunt me for the next 4 years as I try to plot my escape.

After 2 years my drinking is worse and my skin is blotchy under the beard. My scalp has lesions which won't heal. I look a complete wreck. Jenny is fed up and gives me an ultimatum. Either I make a commitment to her and give her a baby or she's going to go back to her parents in Colchester. After five years together that seems reasonable enough, except that I'm an alcoholic with a very uncertain future. Extra responsibility would almost certainly push me over the edge. I decide to have a weeks holiday in Amsterdam to think about it - Jenny goes to stay with her parents for a week.

I am definitely frightened about being on my own - I could marry Jenny just for the stability and the support. I do love her, don't I?

My hotel is a floating 'botel' (a boat hotel) on a canal by Amsterdam's main railway station. It is within walking distance of the red light district. The basic idea for this holiday is to behave badly for a week and then decide if I can sacrifice my freedom for the safety of a permanent relationship.

I am drinking continuously and decide to visit one of Amsterdam's coffee houses to smoke some dope to see if this can replace some of my alcohol consumption. At the coffee house I select something exotic from the menu and light up. When out clubbing, I smoke the occasional cigarette but for some reason I have never become addicted to nicotine (unlike both my parents). Maybe it's my metabolism. I smoke the joint quickly but notice no effect. I order another. Half an hour later, I still feel no different. The pot is expensive and I would rather spend my money on alcohol. I make for the red light area.

A black man approaches me and walks alongside.

"Looking for anything?" he grins.

"Like what?"

"Coke, e, hash?"

I think fast. Pot didn't work for me but maybe coke or an e would. If you hadn't guessed, I am still a bit drunk. I am a bit drunk throughout this week.

"Some coke and e's. How much?" I ask.

"What, coke and e?"

"Yes."

"Three hundred guilders." (That's about 150 dollars.) He shows me a bag of powder and two tablets. He points to a dark alley where we can do the trade. I ignore this and move into the shadows of the main street. We make the trade and I head for an expensive looking hotel I can see in the distance - I need a drink.

As I walk another black man approaches me.

"500 guilders or I'll call the police," he demands.

"What?" I've already realised what's going on but I am stalling hoping to reach the hotel.

"You've got drugs. 500 guilders or I'll call the police."

I stop walking and look at him.

"Go on then." He wasn't expecting this. He looks at me.

"I'll call the police," he affirms. I just look.

"Politie," he says quietly. It's not very convincing. I begin walking toward the hotel again; I've nearly reached it now. The black man gets desperate.

"Politie!" he says. It's almost loud. I drop 50 guilders on the pavement and sprint for the hotel. Over my shoulder I see the man stooping for his money. The doorman opens the door of the hotel as I sprint inside.

"You should be careful of those two," he says, matter of fact. He must have seen the transaction.

"Yes - I worked that out," I reply. In the hotel bar I have a large whisky.

Well, it's cost me a lot of money but I've got my drugs. I decide to go back to my hotel to examine them. Back on the botel, I open the packets. One contains a white crystalline powder, the other two brown chalky tablets. I haven't a clue if it's the real thing. I raid the mini-bar and have another drink. Then I ring my friend Charles who is eight years older than me and has been around a bit. Although he's not a drug user (as far as I know) he may know what to look for.

"Hi Charles, it's me, Paul. I'm in Amsterdam." I tell him the evening's story. On the other end of the phone he's laughing.

"Charles, what should I do with this stuff?" I ask.

"You must be joking," he says.

"What do you mean?"

"The only thing to do with your 150 dollars of stuff is flush it down the toilet. It could be anything."

I think about it. He's right. I thank him for his advice and hang up. Then I go into the bathroom and flush 150 dollars down the toilet.

The next night I decide to get laid. First I go to a bar. The barmaid is a mature but still attractive Asian in an extraordinarily tight pair of slacks which leave nothing to the imagination. I sit at the bar, drink whisky and watch her arse as she moves about serving customers and smiling. She's a flirt. Next to me at the bar is an aging alcoholic who makes me look positively healthy. His hands are bandaged to cover sores and his face is bloated, with broken blood vessels standing out on his cheeks and an enlarged bloodshot nose. He is slurring and only just conscious. He passes out with his head on the bar. Nobody takes any notice.

I am sipping my whisky when I hear a loud crash. Turning, I see that the drunk has fallen off his bar stool onto the floor and his false teeth have come out. I wonder if he is all right; nobody else takes any notice. I get the distinct feeling that he probably does this every night; he still appears to be breathing. Should I try and help him or should I drink my whisky and go and get laid? I drink my whisky, pay my bill and venture out into the night. Yeah, I know, you'd have helped but then you're a fucking Samaritan.

I wander through the red light district and chat to a few girls in their small glass prisons. The going rate for a jump is 50 guilders (30 dollars) for about 15 minutes - not much time for foreplay. I try with a couple of girls but in 15 minutes I just can't get going. I am about to give up and go home when a beautiful, petite, Spanish looking girl with long dark hair waves to me. She is in a white bikini with tanned skin and under the red lighting she looks delectable. She must be 19 or 20. She opens her glass door and practically pulls me inside.

"200 guilders. One hour. I very good." She smiles and licks her lips. I nod and she closes the glass door and pulls a curtain across the glass. Her English is not very good but her body is.

She washes my dick in a basin and begins to caress my balls. Soon I am firm enough for a condom and she begins to lick and suck my genitals. I lie down on the small bed while she climbs out of her bikini. The bed is firm (like my dick) and she hops onto the bed and stands over me. Then she squats down and lowers her pussy onto my dick. Slowly, slowly she bobs up and down, occasionally stopping to smile at me or kiss my nipples. I just lie back and enjoy it. Gently she increases pace and I become more aroused. Visually it's very erotic to see this young tanned girl pleasuring me with her firm body. I reach a peak and climax. She has worked hard and is sweating lightly from the exertion. She kisses my nipples again.

"Thank you Daddy," she says. Some girls just know what to say.

I return to the floating botel and raid the mini bar again. My mind is spinning as I try to make a decision. Stability, security and responsibility with Jenny or freedom, insanity and alcoholism by myself. I ring Jenny at home and propose marriage. She's delighted. I am happy. I ring my parents to tell them the news. They are delighted. I am happy. I sleep.

In the morning I have second thoughts. I spend the next two days drinking, sleeping, worrying, thinking and fucking around. It's nearly time for me to fly home. There's nothing like making a decision to clarify when the decision you've made is the wrong one. I have made the wrong decision. I have proposed to Jenny because I am frightened of being alone. This is not the basis for a marriage, especially when you are an alcoholic in free fall. I ring Jenny.

"Hello Jenny."

"Hello darling." The excitement is still in her voice.

"There's no easy way to say this - I've changed my mind."

Silence. A long silence.

"It's not you, Baby, it's me," I say. This is true. She's a lovely girl and I am a madman. Why she wants me I have no idea - I think she's just got used to me.

"Why?" she asks, almost crying.

"I don't know. I'm an alcoholic. I can't take the responsibility. I'm sorry."

She's heartbroken and I am a bastard. I ring my parents. They are supportive but don't really understand.

Hindsight: I think I made the right decision in the end. Alcoholics don't make good partners and can't handle responsibility.

Life tip: Don't marry an alcoholic.

Chapter 16: Drink the Puke

Back in Manchester, Jenny and I do a deal: she gets the car and I get the cooker and the washing machine. I don't tell her but I am actually very frightened of being alone here. I know my drinking will escalate without her.

She drives off one sunny Saturday morning. I talk to her on the phone a few times but I never see her again. I hear from mutual friends that she's seeing her old boyfriend again and she's pregnant by him. Good for her - she really wants children.

The flat is very empty without her - no surprise there. Work is just desperate. Every lunch time I walk back to the flat and drink vodka. I have a regime. 1/3 bottle of vodka before work, 1/3 bottle at lunch time. After work I buy another bottle and continue drinking until I fall asleep. Sometimes I am so tired at work that I go into a quiet corner of the computer room and sleep for an hour. So far I haven't been discovered.

At the weekend things get silly. I wake up at about 8am and force myself to have a quick shower. I begin drinking vodka and coke while I try to do some housework, or go shopping with a hip flask. I drink continuously until lunch time when I try to eat something before sleeping for 3 or 4 hours. I wake up again in the afternoon at which time I repeat the morning scenario until I fall asleep about midnight. Effectively I split each weekend into four short 12 hour days. During each 12 hour day I drink a bottle of vodka.

Physically buying and carrying this amount of alcohol is a problem. I try to visit different off-licences but it's obvious to most of them that I have a big problem. How I work during the week is beyond me. It's mind over matter. However, this kind of physical abuse can't continue. Every time I drink, I throw up the first tumbler-full as my body tries to reject the poison. I just refill the tumbler and drink again. Every now and then I puke up green bile as my digestive system begins to collapse. It's disgusting. I am disgusting.

I wake up early on a Sunday morning. It's 6am. As I wake up, I remember what I was thinking last night as I fell asleep.

"I don't have enough vodka for the morning."

I was right - there's barely 1/3 bottle left and half of that I'll just throw up. And it's Sunday opening today so I can't buy any more until noon. I am also very ill. There are small spots of fungus growing on my body. Even if I survive today, work tomorrow will be impossible.

I pour the vodka into a glass and add coke. I gulp it down. I have collected a bowl from the kitchen to catch the mixture when it reappears from my stomach. On cue, I puke up. Because I have so little vodka, the idea is to drink the puke. I haven't done this before but I need the alcohol. My body needs the alcohol. I look at the puke in the bowl. I can't face it. I panic. I ring my parents at home.

"I've lost it. I've lost it," I admit tearfully. I explain my situation to my Dad.

"Dial 999 and call an ambulance," he advises.

This seems a bit drastic to me but I do need to go somewhere.

"Call an ambulance," he insists.

"OK, OK, I'll call an ambulance."

I put the phone down and pick it up again. I dial 999.

"Which service do you require?"

"Ambulance." I feel embarrassed.

"Manchester Ambulance Service. What is your address?" I give it.

"What is the emergency, Sir?"

"I need to go to hospital. I am throwing up and I have psychological problems." I think this is true.

"Ok, Sir. An ambulance will be sent. Estimated arrival 15 minutes."

I ring my Dad back and tell him the news. I tidy up the flat as best I can. I have already got the shakes from alcohol withdrawal but my mind is calm. The prospect of an ambulance rushing full tilt to save me seems absurd.

While I wait, I go and look in the mirror and a haggard, sick, alcoholic stares back at me. He has a short unkempt beard and his long hair is tied back in a pony tail. He is chubby and pot-bellied from a long history of drinking. I don't know who he is. I don't recognise him at all.

The ambulance arrives and there is a knock at the door. I open it and two ambulancemen stare at me.

"Where's the patient, Sir?" one asks.

"Er, I'm the patient."

"You can look but don't touch unless I give you permission."

"That's fine with me," I laugh. A sense of humour, she's even got a sense of humour. Tania tells me that she has been living in Britain for about five years, since she was thirty. I cannot believe she is 35 years old. I would have put her in her late twenties.

We have several drinks and then, since we are getting on so well, we decide to go for a meal. In a pleasant Italian restaurant we eat pizza and talk. Tania divorced her husband in Nigeria just before she came to England. He was a government minister but got sacked because there was a change of government, or a coup, or a revolution. Some disaster or another. Now she is living a much less lavish lifestyle and I get the impression that she's looking for a rich boyfriend.

"How much do you earn?" she asks.

"Twenty-three thousand a year."

"Have you got any savings?"

"About ten thousand," I lie. I've really got only three thousand but I rather fancy fucking Tania, if at all possible. She seems satisfied and at the end of the meal I decide to confide in her.

"You realise that I'm an alcoholic?" I say.

She looks aghast.

"Why didn't you tell me before!" She is angry, acting as though I've just confessed to being a serial killer. She wants to leave. I try to persuade her to stay. I tell her I'm trying to change. I pull out my wallet and toss my gold American Express card onto the table next to the restaurant bill. Tania looks at the card, then at me.

"Okay, let's go for a drink and you can tell me about it," she says.

Thank you American Express.

The next night Tania and I arrange a date at the cinema. We meet in the pub next door. Tania is dressed to kill. She is beautifully made up and is wearing knee high boots, a short black skirt and a silver boob tube which barely covers her full breasts. I nearly choke on my drink as she walks over to me.

We talk about my drinking problem and she tells me that her husband was an alcoholic who beat her when he was drunk. That's why she was so angry.

"I'm not violent," I assure her.

We have a few drinks and then take our seats in the back of the cinema. The cinema is quite empty and the film we have chosen turns out to be a bit dull. I begin fondling Tania's breasts under the boob tube and she appears to get a little horny. I fondle her pussy. Then without warning she unzips my fly and begins blowing me. She is an expert.

"I haven't had a fuck for months," she whispers as she comes up for air. "Do you want to fuck me tonight?" Silly question.

I fuck Tania several times over the next few weeks but she is increasingly annoyed at my continual drinking.

"Get clean!" she shouts at me one day. "I don't want to see you again until you are clean."

I don't see Tania for several weeks. Then I get a phone call.

"Paul, its Tania. I have a problem. I need to see you."

We arrange to meet the next Saturday lunch time in a bar. I have been drinking all morning.

"You stink of alcohol," she says. I shrug.

"What's the problem?" I ask. My best guess is that she wants money. Tania wants a better lifestyle and she wants money. My money.

"I'm pregnant," she says. "I need money for an abortion."

I was right. Is she pregnant? Maybe, maybe not. She wants money.

"Go and see a doctor," I say. "You can get a free abortion on the NHS." Yes, I am all heart. Tania is thirty-five years old. She knows how not to get pregnant. We argue for twenty minutes before I get up and leave.

"I'm not giving you any money," I say. She begins to follow me.

"You can follow me all you want. I'm not giving you any money." I go home.

I don't think I'll be going on any more blind dates for a while. Time for a new plan.

Chapter 18: Manchester Tart

Not far from where I live in Manchester is an area frequented by ladies of the night. I am reluctant to use the services of prostitutes in England because it is illegal, completely unregulated and possibly dangerous.

Many of the girls are on drugs and many have diseases. Screwing in back-alleys has never really appealed to me and bringing a girl back to your home poses a whole new set of risks.

However, since I have now given up blind dates my options are limited. I could stay celibate or I could find a whore. After a few large whiskies in my apartment, staying celibate does not seem attractive. I leave my flat and walk twenty minutes to an area just outside the city centre where several unattached young women in skimpy clothes and leather boots have gathered together.

"Looking for business?" says one as I walk past her. I shake my head. She's not very good-looking and too skinny. Many of the girls seem to be either very thin or very fat. None of them are pretty. The thin ones are most likely on drugs, the fat ones are, well, just fat. Amphetamines are a common drug among the girls but it tends to make them boisterous and uncontrollable. They will giggle at nothing and behave unpredictably.

Further down the street I see a mulatto in a short white skirt and a white blouse.

"Looking for business, Sir?" she asks.

She's quite attractive with high cheekbones and a pretty smile.

"Well I might be," I say. "How much to come to my flat?"

"Eighty pounds for an hour," she says.

That's quite expensive but she seems sensible enough and I am very horny.

We get a taxi to my apartment. Inside I pour us some drinks and we talk a little.

"I do this to earn money to support my little son," she says. "I'm not on drugs."

I believe her. I unbutton her blouse to reveal her breasts in a lacy white bra. She has a flat stomach and no stretch marks. It must have been a small baby.

"Where's his father?" I ask.

"He ran out on me when I was five months pregnant. He's an alcoholic."

I begin kissing her while working my hand into her knickers. Conscious of the time, I drain my glass and pour another. Alcohol and testosterone is a heady mixture that loosens my English inhibitions and allows me to fuck. I have had sex stone cold sober but not very often.

"Want another drink?" I ask the girl.

"Yes please."

I pour her another glass.

"Let's go to the bedroom," I say. Time is passing and business is business.

In the bedroom she takes off her boots and sits on the bed. I undress completely except for my briefs and sit beside her. I unfasten her bra and begin sucking on her nipples. I slip her knickers off and feel her pussy. I suck her clitoris until it is hard. Then, rolling a condom onto my hard dick I start fucking her in the missionary position. She closes her eyes. Sex with a girl wearing a short skirt and no knickers is a real turn-on for me. There must be some Freudian reason for it. Maybe it is due to all those games of handstands we used to play in primary school. We boys only used to play the game so that we could see the girls' knickers. Well I did anyway.

After five minutes banging away I know I am going to come. I pull out of her and rip off the condom. I move my body up so that my dick is near her lips. She keeps her eyes closed and closes her mouth instinctively. My ejaculation splashes onto her face and hair. She is not amused.

"You shouldn't have come on me," she chastises. "Now I'll have to go home and wash my hair."

"Sorry," I say. "I couldn't help myself." Well maybe I could have but shit this is costing me eighty quid. When she leaves I give her an extra twenty pounds as a tip.

"Thank you lover," she says. "I hope to see you again soon." All is forgiven.

I repeat the experience with my mulatto once a week for several weeks. I even discover her name. She is called Cheryl. Then she disappears from the streets. Maybe she got a proper job or maybe she left town. The other girls don't know. Cheryl was a nice girl making her way as best she could. I hope she got out of the business and found some happiness but it is a hard business to walk away from.

I can't find a replacement for Cheryl. The other girls all seem to have drug problems and are not really in good health. Instead I decide to visit a massage parlour. Massage parlours exist in Britain and some are completely above board and legal. Most, however, offer additional services that are not so widely advertised.

The massage parlour I find nearest to my home is staffed almost entirely by Asian women in bikinis. Mostly they are from Thailand, smuggled here illegally by criminal gangs who promise them well-paid hotel jobs but instead they are sold onto parlour owners. Their passports are taken away and they are held almost as prisoners until they have earned enough money to buy themselves out of their 'contracts'. They are very keen to buy themselves out.

"Hello, Sir. You like massage?" five small and young Thai women shout in chorus. I look them over. It's a seedy business but then it's a seedy world. Shine a bright light into the nooks and crannies of any apparently legitimate enterprise and the signs of corruption, nepotism, cronyism, dishonesty and double-dealing will be clearly visible. Be certain to ensure your own house is in order before you cast the first stone.

"What's your name?" I ask the girl in the middle. She is the smallest at maybe four feet eleven inches but she has unusually large breasts for a Thai.

"Mikka," she says.

"Well, Mikka, how would you like to give me a massage?"

"Yes please, Sir."

She leads me down a corridor and into a small room containing nothing but a massage table, a wastebasket, a stool and a small coffee table, on which various lotions and potions are visible. Also visible is a large bowl of condoms and a box of tissues.

"Would you like a drink, Sir," Mikka asks.

"Yeah, I'll have a large whisky on the rocks, please." I had a few whiskies before I left home but another one won't hurt.

Mikka leaves to fetch my drink. I sit on the stool and examine the contents of the wastebasket from a safe distance. Unsurprisingly, it contains almost exclusively tissues, empty condom packets and used condoms. This massage is going to cost me fifty quid, plus any extras I want. Shortly I hear the clack, clack of Mikka's sandals as she returns down the corridor. I stand up.

Mikka hands me my drink and immediately begins undoing my belt. She looks at me and winks. I wink back.

The whisky is sharp and tastes good. I down it in one go. Mikka is removing my shoes and socks. Soon I am standing naked except for my briefs. I lie on the massage table on my front and relax as Mikka sets to work. She pours baby oil on me and then begins kneading and rubbing my back, shoulders, arms and legs. She is very professional.

"Turn over now, Sir," she says. She repeats the exercise on my front and is soon rubbing around my groin.

"You want something extra, Sir?"

"How much?" I say.

"Hand job, no condom is twenty pounds. Blow job with condom is fifty pounds. Full sex with condom is eighty pounds. Or my specialty, tit job, no condom is sixty pounds."

Tit job, no condom would definitely be her specialty, I think.

"I'll take a tit job." This is going to work out expensive but you can't take it with you.

Mikka slips off my briefs and begins to rub my dick with her well-oiled hands. Quickly I am very stiff and about to come. Noticing my predicament Mikka stops rubbing and unfastens her bikini top. Her large breasts swing free. She climbs onto the massage table facing me and lets me lick her breasts and suck her nipples. Then she squirts baby oil onto her breasts and kneeling between my legs she positions them over my dick. She slides my hard dick between her oily globes. It feels quite similar to fucking pussy. She is moving up and down faster and faster. I soon feel myself coming.

After she's cleaned us both up with tissues, Mikka goes off and returns with another whisky.

"On the house," she proclaims. I down the whisky and work out the bill. Including a tip for Mikka I owe them nearly two hundred pounds. That really was fun but on 23 thousand pounds a year I can't afford to do it too often.

Chapter 19: The Far East Calls

Several months have passed and I am drinking heavily again. It's the old routine. I am spending a fortune on booze and my savings are dwindling. I've about two thousand pounds left but in six -months that'll be gone. I haven't had a shave. I haven't had a haircut. I haven't got a new job. I haven't been back to see the doctor and I haven't had a shag for so long that I doubt I'd recognise pussy if I saw it.

Fuck it. Fuck it all. Two thousand pounds. I've always fancied a holiday in the Far East. Go out with a bang. Look, holiday in the Far East. Blow two thousand pounds. Get laid if I'm lucky (very lucky from the state of me). Then suicide. It's a cunning plan. I like it. I have even thought of an epitaph for my gravestone. 'Live fast, die middle-aged.'

I call a travel agent who's been advertising holidays in Asia. You know the sort - 'Lads Tours of the Far East Ltd'. I receive a brochure and discover that they are doing a special Philippines and Thailand group tour beginning on 14th October. It's £800 for flight and hotel; eleven nights in the Philippines and 7 nights in Pattaya in Thailand which is supposed to be a beach resort with a hectic night-life.

Today is Saturday August 20th and I begin drinking early. This morning I am on whisky; cheap whisky and by 10am I am feeling sufficiently relaxed. I ring the travel agent and book my place. I hope I am not making a terrible mistake.

It's 14th October; the day of the flight. I have to check in at Manchester airport at 3pm for the 5pm flight to Frankfurt, then it's on to Manila via Bangkok. I am trying not to drink too much. By 1pm I am packed and a little bit merry. I decide to have a nap.

I wake up with a start and look at my watch. Three fucking thirty. Oh my God, it's three fucking thirty. Thank God I'm packed. Frantically I dial for a taxi. I'm sweating and still a bit drunk.

"The taxi will be with you shortly," says the dispatcher.

Fucking marvellous. Look, it's three fucking forty now and it's at least half an hour to the airport and that's if the traffic is light.

I'm sweating profusely when the taxi finally arrives and at the airport the sweat drips off me as I run to the check-in counter carrying my heavy bag. It's four thirty by now and I have no idea if they will let me on the flight.

Oh joy! What relief. I sit back and try to relax in the overly small airline seat I have been assigned. The Far East calls.

The flight is depressing. I don't like crowds. I don't like enclosed spaces. Like most alcoholics I am a bit paranoid. Getting enough to drink to keep me calm on this long flight could be a problem but I have had the foresight to pack a little something extra into my hand luggage. It's a two litre plastic lemonade bottle containing one litre of vodka and one litre of lemonade.

After what seems like forever, we touch down at Ninoy Aquino International airport in Manila. It's late (10pm), very hot and I am overdressed. I badly want a shower. I am met by a bald, overweight guy with a gravely voice and a gravely face. The group leader, George, is in his fifties and slowly he assembles the motley looking group of six individuals he has the dubious pleasure of supervising for the next 18 days.

We are taken by minibus to 'The Jasmine Inn' in the Ermita district of Manila and assigned our rooms. The staff all seems to be gorgeous looking Filipinas. Everywhere I look there are gorgeous looking Filipinas. The Philippines must be full of them. By 11.30pm we are all showered, refreshed and assembled in the reception. George is going to take us to the 'Las Vegas Café', which is a bar not far from the hotel and full of gorgeous looking Filipinas. By now I am starting to get the picture.

The seven of us sit on comfortable stools around the large, circular bar. I am at one end of the group. We order drinks and make introductions. I am the youngest here - that makes a nice change. A gorgeous looking Filipina in a bright red, long, slinky dress and bright red stilettos approaches me.

"Hello Honey, what your name?"

"Paul," I mumble. The other guys are talking amongst themselves, led expertly by George. He has done this many times before.

"Where you from, Honey?"

"England," I say. God she's beautiful. A little bit chubby but she has a beautiful face, no bra and I don't think she's wearing any knickers. I am pleased to find that I instantly recognise the outline of her pussy through the thin material of her dress.

"Where you stay?" she asks.

"The Jasmine Inn," I say. At this she visibly brightens, if she could be any brighter that is.

"Honey, you want good time? 500 pesos. At Jasmine. I suck you, fuck you. 500 pesos, Honey. Yes?"

Five hundred pesos are only about ten dollars. I turn and see that the rest of the group is now all looking at us. I look at George. He shrugs. I think that's the all- clear.

"Suck and fuck for 500 pesos? It's a deal," I say.

Back at the hotel she is true to her word. I am careful and keep the condom on, although I don't think that she was that bothered. I remove the condom, knot it and throw it to the floor. She dresses quickly (she has no panties - just a dress and high heels). I find my wallet and hand over 600 pesos. She has earned it. I give her a kiss and a hug.

"Bye, Honey. Thank you," she calls as the door closes behind her. I soon fall asleep.

In the morning I get a call from George.

"The bus is leaving for Subic Bay in half an hour. Don't be late."

Subic Bay is a large beach area four hours from Manila, which used to be used as a naval base by the Americans. Now it is trying to attract foreign tourists to the beaches and night life and it is here that we are to spend the next 10 nights.

The coach trip to Subic takes ages. The traffic in Manila is wall to wall chaos. Finally we are on the freeway and make better time. The bus has a gorgeous Filipina attendant who serves us cold bottles of San Miguel beer. On the journey George tells me that I might have set a new record for getting laid on one of his group tours.

"I don't think you finished your first drink," he laughs.

"Would the Guinness Book of World Records be interested?" I wonder aloud.

We finally arrive at 'The Nippa Lodge' in Subic at around 3pm. You will not be surprised to learn that the hotel is populated by gorgeous looking Filipinas. One waitress in particular catches my eye as she walks past our group gathered in reception. I quickly read her name tag. Marcia.

Settling into my room, I take a shower. It's so very hot here but the air-conditioning is working efficiently and I soon cool down. We are to meet George in the hotel restaurant at 6pm. By five thirty it is starting to get dark as I walk over the road and into the hotel restaurant. It is a giant Nippa hut and has a very tropical feel to it. I feel at home. I sit at an empty table and a waitress approaches me. It's Marcia. I don't know why I like her, I just do. Maybe it's her smile or her long legs. Maybe it's an air she has about her. I definitely like her.

"Hello Sir, something to drink?" she asks.

"Rum and coke, please Marcia." I smile. I am not a prize by any means but at 36, compared to the rest of the guys in our group, I am practically an Adonis. Marcia smiles back warmly. I think she is interested. Well, why shouldn't she be? I've found out that waitresses in Subic earn about 2 dollars a day. Comparatively speaking, I am a millionaire. Everyone in our group is a millionaire. All foreigners are millionaires. Even ugly, aging, alcoholic millionaires are attractive.

Marcia returns with my drink.

"Can I buy you a drink?" I ask. I already know the answer. Even if I were a homicidal maniac she would let me buy her a drink. Do you know any homicidal maniac millionaires? They are probably attractive too, in their own way.

My drink costs a dollar. Marcia's drink costs two dollars and of that she gets half. That's half a day's pay. As we drink she tells me that she finishes work at eight. Would I like to take her out bar-hopping? This wouldn't happen in England. This couldn't happen in England. Unless I was a real millionaire. The choice isn't difficult. Bar-hopping with 21 year old Marcia or bar-hopping with George and his band of geriatrics.

"I'd love to take you out," I say. "I'll be back at eight."

Back in reception, I see George and explain my plans. He understands. Well, he has seen it all before.

Just after eight, I return to the restaurant. Marcia has changed her clothes. She looks very sexy in low-slung, 70s style, hipster jeans and a bright pink body-hugging top. She has small breasts, no bra and her large, firm nipples are pressing hard on the material trying to break through. Is she wearing any panties? Maybe later, if I am lucky, I'll find out.

Bar-hopping in Subic is fun. Marcia takes me to a few bars and I drink a lot of rum and coke. I am feeling a bit light-headed. In one of the bars there is a stage and dancing girls, wearing bright blue bikinis, gyrate their hips in time to the music. The song playing is a favourite of mine; 'Backstreets Back' by the Backstreet Boys. There are no other customers in the bar so I decide to get on stage and mimic their dance action. I am rather good at it - I like dancing a lot. The girls are all laughing. Marcia is laughing too. Then, someone brings me a spare blue bra and panties. They are the tie-up sort so they could be made to fit. I slip off my shirt and tie on the bra. There is almost a riot. The girls are practically fighting to get a view of me. Spurred on by this, I slip the panties under my own briefs and tie them in place. Then I take off my shorts and underwear. As I sway to the rhythm of the music, the girls clap and the bar owner brings me free drinks. Suddenly, the door opens and George's group bursts into the bar. A star is born in Subic. I never, ever live this down but hell, that's life.

"Do you play pool as well as you dance?" Marcia asks when I finally get my clothes back on.

"Yeah, I love pool." Drinking and pool tend to go together. Most alcoholics can play pool, though not many can dance. Marcia takes me to her favourite bar and I buy drinks for her and her two girlfriends who work there. It's the least I can do and I am still working on the panty angle so I don't want to seem cheap.

Marcia's a good pool player but even drunk I am better. I let her win a few games.

"Shall we bet?" she asks.

"OK," I say. "How much?"

"One frame. 500 pesos. OK?"

This is a lot of money for her. A weeks pay. She must think she can win. I think about letting her win but decide against it. It's a close game but I win on the black. She is upset but hides it well as she hands over the money. I take it from her. She is crestfallen.

We have more drinks. I am trying to find the right moment to give her the money back. Eventually, her friends are playing pool and I seize the opportunity.

"You shouldn't bet what you can't afford to lose," I whisper and slip the folded note unseen into the palm of her hand. She realises immediately what I have given her.

"Thank you, Paul. I love you. Paul, can I stay with you tonight?"

No prizes for guessing my answer.

I am lying butt-naked on my back on top of the bedspread. My dick is rock hard and the condom is already in place. Marcia is standing at the foot of the bed and is naked except for her panties. Slipping out of them, she hops expertly on top of me and guides my dick into her warm, wet pussy. Her nipples are as hard and erect as my dick and nearly as long.

She rides me wildly and it takes all of my willpower to avoid ejaculating. I want to prolong this moment for as long as possible. Finally, it's over and she collapses on me, panting heavily.

"I love you, Honey," she says. I believe her. I am, after all, a millionaire.

Sometimes a change in perspective can help. I decide to stop drinking. I don't need to drink; I am happy. I am in love. I explain things to Marcia and she's marvellous. The first couple of nights it's difficult because I want to drink. I have the shakes and paranoia. Marcia takes me out and protects me. I like to sit and watch her talking to her friends. They speak in Tagalog and I don't understand anything but it's beautiful just to watch them laugh and giggle. I drink coke and sprite. At night Marcia fucks me every which way but loose. It's heaven.

By the end of our ten days together our love has blossomed and my health has improved. In the morning I leave for Manila. I give Marcia 8000 pesos (150 dollars).

"Thank you Granfa," she says as she holds my hands up to her forehead. It's a sign of respect. I don't know that I deserve any. We exchange addresses and I tell her I'll be back in six months. I see Marcia on and off for the next six years.

Chapter 20: Hello Sexy Man

After my eleven days in the Philippines it's time to move on to Thailand. It is only a three hour flight to Bangkok so it is bearable. On the flight George fills me in on the set-up in Pattaya. The bars in Pattaya are mainly 'open' bars gathered together in areas or streets (Soi's). Open means they have no door or walls - they are just a roof over a square bar area. You walk up to the bar and order a drink. Simple as that. Usually there are several bars in a cluster and some of the clusters can be very large. At these bars there are no dancers - just waitresses. If you like one of the waitresses you can buy her a ladies drink or you can pay her bar-fine if she will let you. The bar-fine means she can leave the bar and bar-hop with you. Anything else you want has to be negotiated with the girl.

There are closed bars with dancers too but the drinks are more expensive and so are the bar-fines. The real problem in Thailand is a lack of English. Few of the girls are fluent, so you spend a lot of your time at the bars playing dice games and similar pastimes.

We arrive at the airport terminal in Bangkok around 3pm. It's a 3 hour coach trip to Pattaya but shortly after 6pm I am in my room at the 'Carlton Hotel' getting unpacked.

At 7pm we meet George at reception for a guided tour of the night life. We start drinking at a few open bars in Soi 7, gradually making our way towards the lower Soi numbers where most of the closed bars are.

The only other guy under 50 in our group is Ben. He is 44, muscular and balding with a shaven head. He's a fireman and clearly was once very athletic. He has gone a little to seed but is still attractive in a quiet, macho way. I wouldn't want to mess with him.

I begin talking to him and find out he's been to Pattaya before. We decide to leave the group and explore the closed bars together. We enter a bar called 'The Tahitian'. The bar is dimly lit and a bit dingy. Two girls are playing pool while three others are dancing on a stage. They are not the prettiest girls I have ever seen. Undaunted we order rum and coke and sit at the bar in front of the stage to watch the girls dance. Without Marcia, I can't face the evening sober - sad but true. Two waitresses approach us.

"Hello, what your name?" the one nearest me asks. I tell her.

"Where you from?"

"England," I say. She is flirting with me but I am still sober, I don't fancy her and I just wish she'd go away.

Suddenly, from its hiding place, a giant cockroach about three inches long leaps straight into Ben's nearly full glass on the bar. I look at Ben. He looks at me. I drop a one hundred baht note on the bar to cover the cost of the drinks. We get up and leave.

Further down the street and with a lot more rum and coke inside us we get lucky. In another bar called 'Classroom', where all the girls are dressed in school uniforms, we see a stunningly pretty dancer. Unfortunately we both fancy her. We call her over and buy her a drink. From her body language and her manner it is clear she prefers me to Ben. Probably just because I am younger and have hair. Ben is pissed off but my luck's in - I decide to bar-fine her. However, Ben and I haven't finished getting drunk yet, so I pay the money and tell the girl I'll be back in an hour or so.

We go to a couple more bars; some have dancing girls. In one called 'The Crows Nest', I start talking to the waitress who brought our drinks. She is young (18), cute, with a tight firm body and with all the rum and coke sloshing about in my stomach, I fancy her. We chat some more. I am drunk but functioning and I make a decision - I bar-fine her. Ben can't believe it. He's annoyed because he fancied the first girl.

"OK," I say "Go and find her. If she'll go with you, you can have her."

Satisfied, he leaves the bar and disappears into the night.

It's late now and after buying my new girl a couple of drinks we get a baht bus back to the hotel. In the room we get passionate before I pass out drunk and exhausted. I am woken by Ben banging on my door. My girl is awake and opens the door.

"Are you OK?" asks Ben.

"Yeah, fine," I manage to say - my head is reeling from too much rum.

"Check your wallet," he says.

I check - it's all in order.

"That's a relief," says Ben. Apparently, on his way to his room he saw my girl at my room door talking to one of the night porters and he was worried she was rolling me. I am too drunk to care and quickly fall asleep again.

In the morning I wake Ben and we decide to take our girls for a late breakfast across the street. When we are all dressed we meet at reception. Ben's girl is very cute behind the sunglasses she is wearing. She has a very pretty smile.
"Where did you find this one?" I ask. She really is attractive.
"It's your first one from last night, stupid," he says. I try hard to remember. This girl looks much prettier than the girl I am vainly trying to picture in my head.
Over breakfast, Ben is persistent and whispers to me.
"Why did you go with the second girl?" He still can't believe I bar-fined the second girl. Nor can I.
"I liked the second one," I whisper back.
"Come on, why did you go with the second one?" he whispers again.
"Look, I just liked the second one."
"I don't believe you. Why did you bar-fine the second one?" He is raising his voice now and I am worried the girls will hear. I have a rule. If someone asks me a question three times I assume they want a truthful answer. I whisper in Ben's ear.
"I asked her if she took it up the arse and she said yes."

The next evening I decide to go bar-hopping alone. Last night's girl was fun and pretty but her English was poor and even with the help of my Thai-English pocket dictionary, communication was difficult. I really want to find a girl I can hold a conversation with.
I am wandering in the large bar complex at Soi 9, listening to the cries of "Hello sexy man!" from the girls trying to attract customers to their bar. The noise from the many music systems is at times deafening. I pass one bar and see a very slim, petite girl with short bobbed hair. She is wearing a short white dress and she is perched precariously on a pair of extremely high white stilettos.
I sit on a bar stool and order a drink while watching the girl talk to another customer at the far side of the bar. She shakes his hand and he wanders away into the crowd. I call to the girl.
"Hey. Can I buy you a drink?"

"Sure," she says as she totters over to me. "How are you? My name's Bing." She offers her hand for a handshake. Her English seems good.

"Hello Bing. I'm Paul," I say, while taking her very small soft hand in mine. "Who was the other guy?" I ask.

"Oh him. He's just a customer. He's just paid my bar-fine. I meet him at his hotel in three hours."

Damn. She's already bar-fined and I really like her.

"Do you fancy a short-time with me?" A short-time is basically a quick fuck.

"Yeah okay," she says. "Where are you staying?"

"The Carlton."

"Let's go," she says, grabbing her bag from under the counter.

At the hotel we fuck. Her pussy is completely hairless and naked she is delectable. She is also enthusiastic, moaning at the attention of my tongue and sucking happily on my dick. I let her suck my dick without a condom just so that when her next customer kisses her he can taste my dick. Yes, I am a bastard. Finally I bang Bing to a climax. We lie exhausted on the bed for an hour until she has to go.

"My next guy will be waiting. I must go now." She begins dressing.

"OK. I'll come and see you tomorrow. I want you to stay with me long-time."

"That's good. See you tomorrow." With a wave she's gone. Off to her next assignation.

The next evening I arrive early at Bing's bar. She's wearing jean hot pants, a tiny white T-shirt and plain white trainers. She runs over and gives me a big kiss. I am probably kissing the other guy's dick but at least she should have brushed her teeth in the meantime.

"Hello Honey, I'm so glad to see you," she enthuses. "The guy last night was a jerk. I'm glad he only wanted short-time."

"I'm glad you're here too Bing. I think you're really cute."

I spend most of the next seven days and nights with Bing. Either in the hotel swimming pool, lazing on the beach or drinking in the bars. She's good fun to be with, she can play pool and she speaks quite good English. She's not Marcia though and I haven't been able to refrain from drinking.

She tells me that she has a French boyfriend supporting her and soon she hopes to marry him and go to live in France. I bet he doesn't know that she's still working. Still, what he doesn't know won't kill him, will it?

As I climb onto the coach that is to take us back to Bangkok airport I hand Bing several thousand baht.

"Thank you Honey," she says. "Take care."

I watch her waving at me until the coach turns a corner and she is out of sight. Tonight she'll be back at the bar looking for a new customer. But still I love her and I wish her well.

Chapter 21: Fucking Crazy

Returning to Manchester, I make a decision. I've got to get another job. This job is making me ill. The stress is too high, the work is unorganised, the bosses are, for the most part, ignorant. I study C & Unix again, working hard in any spare time I've got. I shave off my beard. My skin is blotchy but improving. I get a haircut. My scalp still has lesions but they are improving too. I still binge drink on Friday or Saturday night, but it is manageable.

After 5 months, I decide it is now or never. My employment contract has a 3 month notice period, which is a fucking liberty (I am not management) and probably legally unenforceable. It makes me unattractive to new employers who don't want to wait that long for a new employee. Fuck them all. I write my letter of resignation. I have already planned a two week holiday in the Philippines for the start of the second month of my notice period. I hand deliver my letter. My old boss Phil has left Imasys by now and my new boss hates my guts. He reads the letter. He is angry (he needs me) and happy (he hates my guts).

I don't have a new job to go to but I don't care. I'm getting out of this hell-hole and going back to my house in Colchester. My tenant is leaving shortly so my house will be available. If I can't get a new job, the endgame is to sell the house, move in with my parents (they don't know this) and live off the equity until my luck changes. The final endgame is, of course, suicide but now I have Marcia so suicide isn't an option, is it?

I keep a low profile at work for a month and then escape to the Philippines. Marcia and I have been corresponding for the last six months and we have a great reunion. It's as good as before, if not better. We talk about getting her a visa to visit me. It's difficult, expensive and the British embassy don't want to play ball. The two weeks is up and I have to return home but I tell Marcia that I will persist and write to the embassy from England.

Back in Manchester, I turn up for work at Imasys.

"We didn't think you'd be coming back," laughs my boss. At the end of the day, I pack my things and leave without a word. I never go back.

I hire a car and shuttle my belongings back to my Colchester house. It's good to be home but I am worried because I still can't get a job. I drink Friday nights and Saturdays but not heavily. Not for me.

Scanning the computer press, I see what I have been looking for: C, Unix programmers wanted by Marconi in Chelmsford - 25K. Not a lot of money but Chelmsford is only about 30 minutes from Colchester by train and I can walk to Colchester train station from my house in about fifteen minutes. I ring the agent. They want to interview me and test me on C and Unix before sending me on to see their client.

The next day I put on my one suit, hire a car and drive to their office in St. Albans. The interview goes well. I am sober and attentive. Then it's the computer based test. I do well enough. The client (Marconi) will see me in two days time.

I get the train to Chelmsford. Marconi's New Street factory complex is right by Chelmsford's station. My luck's in - the commute is reasonable. Almost easy. After a quick introduction to the company by the human resources department, the prospective employees (there are 5 of us) are led one by one to our interviews by management. I am interviewed by John Coster. He is a Marconi veteran, grey-haired, a little dishevelled, intense blue eyes. I like him immediately.

He tells me about the system they are writing. They have an international team of engineers spread across three sites - Chelmsford, Borehamwood in London and somewhere in Italy. Together these teams are building a leading edge managed network system for HF radio. No one has successfully implemented such a system before although several companies have tried. It's an 80+ man year project for the Swedish armed forces and is known as KV90. It is over half a million lines of code already and is two years and five million pounds over budget. They have got to be joking. This will never work. International teams spread across three sites. Fucking crazy.

"Do you want the job?" John asks.

They are fucking crazy.

"Yes, count me in, John."

I start a week later and work frantically. This is a very professional setup. The best software engineers I've ever worked with - better than Philips, even. But they are building a state of the art system and things are not going well. The international spread of the teams is a huge handicap. Eventually, the Italians deliver their database code and disappear from the project.

The system still does not work.

The team in Borehamwood is moved to Chelmsford. All the engineers are now working at one site so communications between teams becomes easier.

The system still does not work.

I survive at Marconi for eighteen months and am promoted to become one of the team leaders. Then I begin looking for another job - the work has become repetitive and frustrating and I am underpaid.

The system still does not work.

I hear later that it takes another 2 years and £7 million to get the system to work. KV90 finds service with the Swedish army in the Kosovo peace mission.

I find a new job at a software house in Chelmsford. They will pay me five thousand pounds a year more than I was getting at Marconi to help write an insurance system for a major British insurance company.

I arrive for my first day at work to discover I have made a big mistake - they are a badly organised rabble. One recent new recruit walks out in less than three months. Another is fired, while I search for a lifeboat. It is this kind of stress that can drive a man to drink but I resist the temptation. With my C and Unix experience, I am now pretty employable.

I ring a Chelmsford company called Netforce who specialise in internet systems. After two interviews we strike a bargain and I add another two thousand pounds to my salary (32K now). I am very interested in working on internet systems but they are very interested in my Marconi real-time messaging experience (KV90).

One of Netforce's key employees is a Dutch guy called Pieter from Rotterdam, who has written a real-time messaging system for a company in Oldham. The system is written in Microsoft technology (Visual Basic and Access97), which I know virtually nothing about. The system works but has problems and needs to be upgraded. Unfortunately for Netforce, Pieter wants to go back to Holland and has already resigned. He has only two weeks left to hand the system over to someone. Me.

Pieter is a young computer science wizard and has spent about 18 months writing this system - it is very complex. It was supposed to take only 3 months to write (young computer science wizards aren't generally very good at estimating) so it is hugely over budget and the customer is unhappy. He wants his upgrade as fast as possible.

Pieter has been much too busy to write documentation, so I try to figure out what the system does by looking at the code. I quickly realise it will be impossible to understand it in just two weeks.

"Pieter, it's not possible for me to take this over in two weeks is it?"

"No," admits Pieter, "but that's your problem."

It's good to know who's on your side.

To take over a system, the minimum requirements are:
1) Be able to test it working.
2) Be able to make changes and compile them.
3) Be able to test your changes and debug any problems.

I focus on these three areas and leave the code until later. If necessary, I will pick the code apart line by line until I know what each one does. This would clearly take several months.

After two weeks Pieter leaves. I am able to perform the three tasks listed above. Six months later the upgrade is installed. It is a great success but my boss is not happy because it has taken so long. To be honest, he's an arrogant, ignorant git and I don't like him. I also find out that he's earning about £80 thousand a year, which is about double what he would get at any other company. There must be some office politics going on here and I am on the outside. I resolve to change jobs as soon as practicable.

My boss assigns me to a new project. The deadline is frankly impossible or at the very least unrealistic. He expects me to work overtime for nothing to produce the goods. I tell him to "Fuck Off" but rather more politely.

I have been working on the new project for about a month and I am behind schedule. Out of the blue, my boss calls for a 'code review'. A code review is essentially a meeting where the programmer explains his code line by line to interested parties for constructive criticism. It's supposed to reduce the number of bugs in the final code. At Marconi we had them all the time and they are very helpful in ensuring a robust product. In all the history of Netforce there has never, ever been a single code review before. I smell a rat.

In order to try and stay on schedule, I have taken some coding shortcuts to get the system working. I intend to clean the code later and I explain this at the code review. Some constructive comments are made.

The next day my boss calls me into his office and hands me a letter. It's an ultimatum. Either I clean the code and get back on schedule in my own time or I face the consequences. 'Be prepared' is my motto, if you remember. I reach into my pocket and pull out a letter of my own. It's my resignation. I have been carrying it around for several weeks. I date it, sign it and hand it to him. Fuck you sonny, I think (he's several years younger than me) - you're playing with the grown ups now. Plus I'm stone cold sober.

Chapter 22: Consultancy Sucks

Back at home, I have a new full-time job. It's called job hunting. I've pretty much exhausted the Chelmsford job market, so I start looking farther afield. I put my house on the market - I'll probably have to move. I finally get an interview with Computer Sciences Corporation (CSC), a big American computer services company. They have 50,000 employees worldwide and 5,000 in the UK. Their consultancy division, based in Farnborough, employs 1000 people and they are looking to expand. The new area of their interest: the Internet.

I talk up the Internet experience I gained at Netforce. Also I've been studying the Internet programming language called Java in my own time for the last couple of years, so I can talk a good Java story. They are interviewing a lot of people but, surprisingly, I convince them I know my stuff and they offer me a job. The package is worth around £40 thousand and is to be based in Farnborough. This is not a lot of money for a forty year old programmer with twenty years of development experience. Unless, of course, you're an unemployed forty year old programmer.

I work out some logistics. During the week I can live with my brother in Hammersmith (West London) - he has a room available to rent in the house-share where he lives with his girlfriend. I have a company car, so the 45 minute drive from Hammersmith to Farnborough is manageable. At the weekend I can drive the three hours back to Colchester and live in my house. I still can't seem to sell it but I have had quite a lot of viewings.

I get bad news from the Philippines. Despite my best efforts with the British embassy in Manila, I have been unable to get Marcia a visa. She emails me from Subic and tells me that she has met a 31 year old American who is serving in the U.S. Air Force based in Korea. She has a licence to marry him and she's got a U.S. visa. She's sorry but she's going to Korea.

It's not entirely unexpected - the last time I visited her in Subic, she got drunk once and told me there was someone else interested in her. I am upset, but it's her future she's thinking of. She's 25 now and in a hurry to make something of her life. From her point of view it makes perfect sense. The effect she has had on my life has been enormous. It was with her that I discovered how to enjoy myself and stay sober. The fact that she's now out of my life is worrying - I hope I don't start to spiral out of control again.

My first week working for CSC is an induction course at an expensive hotel. My health has improved and I look the part of a computer consultant, with a new suit and now quite close cropped hair. There is a group of about 15 inductees and I am towards the upper end of the age range. I don't really like this sort of gathering - I like computers, not small talk and horse-shit. Over the next 8 months at CSC I am going to become very familiar with horse-shit - it is the stock in trade of the consultant.

The other problem with this kind of induction week is the pressure to socialise and drink. You put 15 strangers in a hotel for 24 hours a day and compel them to pretend to like each other. You then force-feed them a diet of team building, bonding and company horse-shit. I spend every evening in the bar drinking. So does everyone else.

One evening we are all assembled in the bar for a drinking game. Shortly into the game I come to my senses, tell the leader I have a migraine and go to bed. The next morning at breakfast I feel OK - the others look terrible. Drinking games are almost never a good idea and not recommended for recovering alcoholics.

Life tip: If you are an alcoholic, do not indulge in drinking games.

I emerge almost unscathed from the induction week and I have learned something useful. CSC is full of horse-shit.

At work, I am surprised to find I know my new colleagues, Henry and James. Both interviewed me when I applied for this job. I didn't realise at the time that I would be working with them. Henry is a black doctor (academic not medical) eager for promotion and happy to toe the company line. He is already a senior consultant and the project manager for this development. Henry is not technical. James is a young Java consultant who is surprisingly cynical about CSC. You will probably immediately guess that I like James enormously.

James is one of the two programmers already working on this project but he is going on holiday for two weeks, so Henry instructs me to ring the other developer, Gary, to determine what I should do first.

James and Gary have written a prototype of a demand forecasting system, which is to be deployed on an intranet at Dupont. It is all written in Java but the prototype is rudimentary and needs a lot of work. I ring Gary. He is based in Leeds - this is another project suffering from multi-location syndrome.

"I don't care what you work on," he says. "I'm too busy working on the server here and my wife's having a baby so I can't come down and talk to you."

"Fucking marvellous," I think.

I spend the two weeks working on the GUI (Graphical User Interface) software that James has been writing and ignore Gary. I will spend the next 8 months trying to ignore Gary.

James returns from holiday and is impressed by what I've accomplished. We split the work up. I'll continue writing the GUI client. We'll leave Gary doing the server software. James will try and get the two to talk successfully to each other. That means he has to talk to Gary. I don't.

To complicate matters, there is another project manager on the scene. He is Colin and he is the guy from Dupont. Colin really just gets in the way - he doesn't know anything except he knows his ass is on the line if we screw up. We try to leave Colin to Henry - they have heated arguments.

After a couple of months, we seem to be making progress. And there is good news on the home front. A young couple has made an offer on the house and after a bit of negotiation we settle on a price of £77,500. It's less than I wanted but a fair price and after paying off the mortgage and the legal fees etc, I should be left with a cheque for about ten thousand pounds. That's around 1,000 bottles of cheap whisky or two and a half years drinking money.

I arrive for work early one Monday morning and have a very unexpected email. It's from Marcia. She is now in America - her husband has been transferred to an air base in Mississippi. However, they are not getting on and she says she is missing me.

My pulse is racing as I email her back. Eventually she sends me her phone number and I ring her every week. We become very close again. I am already aware that there is a huge shortage of Java engineers in the U.S. because the internet is booming. I start sending my resume to U.S. recruitment agencies.

The system is slowly taking shape but I am finding it increasingly hard to believe that it will ever do anything really useful. It is a demand forecasting system that is being written on the basis of a few mock-up screen-shots produced by Colin. And he keeps changing his mind about what he wants. Where's the beef? James is also depressed. I think he has similar doubts and he leaves CSC to take a job for less pay and stock options. Everyone wants stock options now.

I am promoted to GUI team leader and get a new enthusiastic but inexperienced recruit. In Leeds Gary has become server team leader and has a helper also. The good news is I am a team leader, the bad news is I have to talk to Gary on the phone.

Gary keeps changing the server software without telling me and then blaming me because the GUI software doesn't work. Henry gets involved. Gary is adamant that the problem is on the GUI, not the server. I am sure the problem is on the server. Henry believes Gary; Henry and I have a difficult relationship. We have a teleconference and Gary starts examining the GUI code remotely from the Leeds office. He keeps picking holes.

"Look, Gary - nothing has changed on the GUI. Not a thing. You must have changed the server."

"I haven't," Gary insists. He has not found a fault with the GUI and is now rechecking his own server code. Suddenly he goes quiet.

"OK, I think I may have found a problem." Gary breaks his silence.

"I'm sorry Gary, what did you say - I didn't quite catch it." I am dancing around the office but Gary can't see this.

"I said I think I have found a problem on the server."

"I am surprised," I say sarcastically, while grinning victoriously at Henry. He is not amused.

Later, when the project is over, Henry writes my project evaluation.

"Not a team player," says his report.

Fuck you, Henry - it doesn't matter what you think, my American agent has got me a years contract in San Francisco. All it took was a twenty minute phone interview with the client.

I'm not sure if the system installed at Dupont ever did anything useful. Probably just gathered dust. I am glad to be getting out from under all this CSC horseshit.

I send out the following email to all my CSC colleagues:

Paul Pisces/UK/CSC
03/03/2000 09:39
To: UK/CSC
cc:
Subject: Ooooooh Eer Missus
Hello Everybody,

I'm the dude who used to wear a dodgy blue cardigan (and at one time was aka 'super-cardigan man') and who has recently been sporting a loud, tasteless series of waistcoats.

Today is my last day at CSC, not because of my poor sartorial style but because I've been offered a contract to work for a dot com in San Francisco.

The decision to go or stay was a close call - I am after all a natural masochist or I wouldn't be here.

However, I wish you all the best of luck.

God speed; God bless.

In life it's not the surface but the substance that matters.

-Paul

My U.S. work visa has arrived and I am to fly out on March 16th. I will spend my 41st birthday (March 18th) in America.

Chapter 23: San Francisco Millionaires

I am to be paid $65 an hour - that's about $150K for a years contract or around £100K. Anyway you look at it, that's quite a lot of money. It's a risk, however, because they could fire me at any time and this internet bubble could burst. Right now, in March, the NASDAQ is over 5000 and still rising. However, I'm going to keep my £10K in the bank.

Prices in San Francisco are exorbitant. I rent a one bedroom apartment near Pier 38 with a very nice view of the bay. It costs $2500 a month. Shit. It is comfortable though, and the apartment complex has a free shuttle bus service to the financial district where I will be working, so I don't need to rent a car.

On the first day of the contract (Monday 20th March), I am collected by my American agent Scott and taken to the client's address. Scott also took me out on Saturday for my birthday and bought me a fancy meal - well he has got to do something for his commission.

The offices at Buzzsaw.com are bursting at the seams with desks squeezed into meeting rooms and even corridors but it seems well organised and my desk, laptop, phone and userids are all ready for me. I am working in a meeting room with two other guys. We are all to work on the same part of Buzzsaw's web site - the marketplace. Dave is an intense 30 something programmer with a high opinion of himself and his ability. Mike is younger (late 20s). He is an Englishman who has been in the States with his wife for four years already and he is desperately waiting for his green card to give him permanent resident status. He also has a high opinion of his ability. I reserve judgement.

The marketplace software is from a company called Ariba. They are one of the darlings of the NASDAQ at the moment with a share price of $150 and a price-to-earnings ratio of several hundred. Madness really.

After a week getting familiar with the software, I am looking forward to relaxing at the weekend. Scott wants to take me out on Friday night to show me around town. I like Scott, at least he's making an effort to help me settle in - maybe he's actually worth his commission.

Scott picks me up at the office at 5pm and we begin driving to the restaurant. A call comes in on his car-phone and Scott answers it.

"Do you know where Paul is?" I can just hear the voice on the phone's speaker. It is urgent and harassed and belongs to my new boss Julia.

"He's with me," Scott answers, composed and smooth. After years of work as an agent, this is automatic - he is always composed and smooth.

"Look, Ariba have a cancellation for their training course which starts on Monday. We want Paul to fly out to Tampa on Sunday and attend the course," Julia continues.

Scott looks at me. I nod enthusiastically - Tampa is in Florida and I haven't come all this way to miss out on free trips around the States. Plus training makes you more useful and less likely to be sacked.

Over Saturday the arrangements are made and on Sunday I get a taxi to San Francisco's main airport for the flight to Tampa. In Tampa, I hire a car, make the short five minute drive to the hotel and I am all set for Monday morning's training course.

I arrive early at Ariba's offices for the course - this is likely to be stressful enough without being late. I had a couple of beers last night with my meal but it really was only two. American office hours are generally 8 - 5 with an hour for lunch but the course is due to start at 9am.

I wait patiently in the offices but at 9am there are still no other participants and no trainer. I talk to reception again and finally the training manager arrives for work and is summoned. I explain why I am there.

"But that course is being held in Atlanta, Georgia," she tells me.

Not only am I in the wrong city - I am in the wrong state. What a fuck up. I ring my boss's mobile number. I am on the east coast of the States and it is only 6am on the west coast. Despite being woken up she is very reasonable though still harassed.

"Yes, yes. I'm sorry. Someone's messed up. Just fly to Atlanta, hire a car. Anything. We'll pay."

Ariba's training manager helps make the arrangements. There's a first-class seat available flying from Tampa to Atlanta at noon. It will arrive at 2.30pm in Atlanta. I rush back to the hotel to check out and manage to make the flight. I lie back in my first class seat and try to relax. I resist the temptation to order a large whisky. My stress level, pulse rate and blood pressure must be off the scale. In Atlanta it is a one hour drive to the training site. I hire a car. I am driving on the wrong side of the car, on the wrong side of the road, with unfamiliar street signs and I am very sure that I am going to get lost or have an accident.

I finally arrive in the training classroom just after 4pm. I am absolutely exhausted. The other participants are performing the final exercise of the day, so the lady trainer, who has been warned of my arrival, spends an hour briefing me on what they have been covering on this first day. That night in my hotel room, I read the documentation I have been provided with. I don't sleep well.

The final afternoon of the course there is a test. If you fail the test you receive an "Attended Course" certificate. If you pass the test you receive a "Completed Course" certificate. I don't know if it matters to Buzzsaw whether I pass this test or not, but I don't want to take any chances. The examination consists of a written paper followed by a practical test, modifying code. None of it is straightforward and I missed the first day of class.

I manage to pass the written paper - now for the practical. It's 2pm and I am becoming very aware of the time. My flight from Atlanta to San Francisco is at 5.30pm, so I must leave the training course by 4pm at the very latest. The practical test is difficult. The trainer is bombarded by questions from all the participants and she is unhappy and over-stretched.

I can't get my changes to work. The debugger won't run and it's 3.30pm. I run through the instructions again. Finally by some miracle the debugger springs to life and I pore over the output. I find my bug. A quick change, a recompile and I run the code. It works. It fucking works. I interrupt the trainer in mid-sentence, grab her by the arm and force her to watch my now working code. She issues me with a "Completed Course" certificate. I run for the door. I am the first to leave. Behind me I leave a dozen individuals in differing states of despair.

Back at Buzzsaw, talking to my colleagues, I discover that there are very few contract workers and the permanent staff all have relatively low salaries but huge stock options. They cannot believe I haven't got stock options.

"Everyone's got stock options and we're going to IPO (Initial Product Offer) on the NASDAQ in July or August. We're all going to be millionaires." Dave is serious. Everyone is serious. They are all going to be millionaires by the summer. All except me.

In April the NASDAQ collapses. Big time. Stocks halve in price or worse. Some lose 90% or more of their value. There are many stories of people who have lost millions. The Buzzsaw IPO is postponed but the crash is seen as a temporary blip and normal service will be resumed by the Autumn.

"We'll all be millionaires by Christmas," is the new cry, although I notice people seem to be a little more envious of the comparatively large salary I squirrel away in the bank every month.

After a couple of months, I buy Marcia a plane ticket to come and visit me. She will stay with me in San Francisco for a week and then fly on to see her aunt in Virginia. She only tells her husband about visiting her aunt.

Late one Friday afternoon in June, I meet Marcia at the airport - it's been nearly two years since we last saw each other. At first she doesn't recognise me. I am thinner because I have lost some of the beer gut I gained while drinking so heavily. Then she sees me and smiles. She's changed too - older, more mature, more composed but still beautiful. We embrace. It's just like old times. After a hesitant start we are soon talking like old friends. I can't take my eyes off her nipples - they haven't changed.

She is impressed by my waterfront apartment and equally impressed by the excellent restaurant I take her to a couple of hours later. The restaurant is a two minute walk from my flat and is called the Delancy Street Café. Interestingly enough it is part of the Delancy Street Project, which is a rehabilitation complex for recovering alcoholics, drug addicts and petty criminals. I feel very at home here. The service is fast and efficient, the food is good value and I understand the staff - they have been where I have been.

We have a lovely meal and a bottle of wine between us. Marcia is flirting with me suggestively. I haven't had a fuck for months;

years even. It is worth waiting for. Back at the apartment we christen the rented bed.

I bang Marcia at least fourteen times during the week she's with me. After all, I do want to get value for the money I spent on the plane ticket. The next Saturday I take her to the airport for her flight to Virginia. On the way we make plans.

"As soon as I get my green card I will come and stay with you," she promises. She should get this within another 6 months. If she leaves her husband before this she may be deported back to the Philippines. Every week we talk on the phone.

Chapter 24: Lady-Man

With Marcia back in Mississippi, I am at a very loose end in the evenings. I decide to try Internet dating. I register with the AOL dating service and scan through the females of San Francisco who have also registered. I send a few attractive girls a message and then I come across a more unusual posting. It is from a twenty-five year old Thai male transsexual called Cherry. From the photograph he/she looks very pretty. It's Saturday evening and I am a bit drunk. I send Cherry a message.

In Thailand there are many extremely beautiful transsexuals known as lady-men. They have breast implants and hormone treatment. A few have had their genitals surgically removed. It is often hard to believe that they are not women. Straight men have been known to bar-fine them and only discover that they are not women once they are in bed. They reach down and start feeling for pussy - instead they get a handful of dick.

The tips I was given when I was in Thailand on how to recognise lady-men are:
1) If she is very, very beautiful then she is a lady-man.
2) If she has a large Adam's apple then she is a lady-man.
3) If she has long fingers then she is a lady-man.
4) If she has big feet then she is a lady-man.
5) And finally, if, when you are in bed together, you reach down and get a handful of dick then she is a lady-man.

I have never been with a lady-man although, if I found a really pretty one, I might be tempted.

My AOL lady-man emails me back with her phone number. She appears keen to meet. I drink half a bottle of vodka, summon up all my Dutch courage and ring the number.

"Hello." A slightly effeminate voice with a Thai accent answers the call.

"Hello. Is that Cherry?" I ask.

"Yes, this is Cherry. Who's calling?"

"I'm Paul. I emailed you yesterday."

"Well, hello Paul. It's good to talk to you. Would you like to meet?"

"Yes OK. What about tonight?" I say.

"Meet me at the entrance to the Embarcadero centre at 8pm. I know a nice restaurant we can go to."

"OK, I'll see you there."

By 7pm I am having second thoughts. This could be a very bad idea. Nevertheless I get myself ready and catch the metro to the Embarcadero. After all, Cherry doesn't know what I look like. If I see her and don't like the look of her I can just walk past. And anyway, this is San Francisco. Everyone's gay. In fact you're a bit of an outsider if you're straight.

I arrive at the Embarcadero centre just after 8pm. Cherry is standing outside and looks stunning. She is petite at five feet four and is wearing a little black dress and black high heels. She has a gold necklace and delicate gold bracelets on both wrists. I introduce myself.

"Hello Paul. You are just gorgeous," she says.

"I was just thinking the same thing about you," I say.

She is well made up and looks very feminine. As I shake her hand I check her fingers. They are small. I check her feet. Small too. I check her Adam's apple. Hardly visible. However, she is very, very beautiful.

Cherry takes me by the hand and leads me towards Market street.

"Let's go to my favourite restaurant," she says. "It's my treat." As we walk I study her for any masculine traits but I can't see any. The restaurant is called 'Merlins' and at the entrance there is a heavy metallic door. Cherry rings a bell and the door is swung open from the inside. As we enter I soon realise why Cherry likes this restaurant. It is full of transvestites. The waitresses are transvestites, the bar staff are transvestites. I am not sure if the chefs are transvestites but it wouldn't surprise me. Not all the customers are transvestites but many are.

We are guided to a table near the bar area and I take a while to look around. I am pleased to find that I am with the prettiest transvestite here.

"This is an unusual place," I say.

"Yes, I love it here." Cherry smiles.

I rather like it too.

"Later there will be a show," Cherry says.

We order our food from an Asian/American menu and drink Margaritas while we wait for the appetisers to arrive. The food is good. Our waitress is rather butch and certainly wouldn't fool anybody into thinking she was really a girl. In fact very few of the transvestites would pass as women even with only the most cursory of inspections. Thai transvestites are definitely the best in the world.

As our main course arrives the stage-show starts. It consists of a parade of some better looking transvestites miming to well known pop records. It is entertaining and very camp. I have to try very hard not to laugh.

"You can laugh if you want," says Cherry, noticing my amusement. "We don't take ourselves too seriously, you know."

I shriek with laughter and everybody in the restaurant looks over at our table.

"I said laugh, not shriek," says Cherry, trying to suppress her own giggles.

Our meal is over and Cherry picks up the bill. She refuses to let me pay anything.

"There is one thing you could do for me," she purrs, as we leave the restaurant. We are both a little drunk…...

Chapter 25: Herds of Homeless

San Francisco is a bizarre contradiction. A city with one of the highest per capita incomes in the world and it is full of homeless people. At the eastern end of Market Street near the bay and the ferry port is the Financial District. At the other end of the street is the Loin area, where, at night, herds of homeless people pushing shopping carts full of their few belongings gather together to build small cardboard houses on the pavements. Other homeless people sleep in shop doorways on cardboard mats. The pavements at night smell of urine and they are hosed down every morning by an army of workmen.

During the day many of the homeless pan-handle for change. They are not usually aggressive but they are a constant reminder of a huge forgotten proportion of the population who have fallen through the almost non-existent welfare net of the U.S.A. To be fair, a lot of homeless people are attracted to San Francisco because the climate is good all year round and the people are generally generous to beggars. But it is hard to believe that at least some basic services couldn't be provided to help these people get off the streets.

Accommodation is another problem for San Francisco. There is very little affordable housing and even the undesirable neighbourhoods are expensive. You need to be earning a good salary not to be homeless.

The homeless are not just alcoholics, drug-addicts and people with mental health problems. There are mothers and babies and even families.

I decide to walk home from work one evening in order to do some shopping in a local store not far from my apartment. I purchase my goods and step outside. I see a young black couple with two small children walking toward me. There is nothing out of the ordinary about them. They look as if they are out for an evening stroll.

The woman comes up to me and says something. I think she must be asking for directions.

"I'm sorry," I say. "I didn't hear you."

"I wondered if you could spare us some money," she says.

I look in her eyes. She is embarrassed, sad and desperate. I can't think of what to say. How can I help a family? How much money to help a family? Five dollars? Ten dollars? A hundred dollars?

"I'm very sorry, I can't help you," I say. I really am very sorry. I often give ten dollars to a down and out if I am in the mood and that can at least ease his existence for a short while. But how do I help a family?

"Have a nice day," says the man genuinely.

I think a family like this will get help as soon as they find the right government agency but it is sad to think that amidst such extraordinary wealth there is such an ordinary family out on the streets asking strangers for money.

Chapter 26: New Orleans Blues

It's been three months since I've seen Marcia so I decide to fly to New Orleans for a long weekend. I have booked Monday as a holiday so that I will be able to spend at least two nights with her. There is one obvious difficulty with this plan - her husband. Marcia says this shouldn't be a problem because she can visit me in the evening and return home by 2am. She will tell her husband that she is going out with her girlfriends.

I arrive in New Orleans on Saturday afternoon to discover that it is baking hot. Earlier I had rung Marcia from Houston, where I had to change planes, and I am relieved to find her waiting for me outside the airport terminal. We kiss and hug. She assures me that there will be no problem seeing me tonight as she drives me to a large casino-based hotel just outside the city in Mississippi. Air conditioning in Mississippi appears to be mandatory. The cars have it, the restaurants have it, the hotels have it, the cafes have it. Even the telephone kiosks have it. Marcia drops me at the hotel and I say I will ring her later.

The hotel is huge. On the ground floor there is a vast gambling area with slot-machines, blackjack tables and roulette wheels. Hordes of gamblers gather around the tables or cruise between them. Mostly they are the older generation (even older than me). I have played blackjack before but gambling has never really appealed to me. I prefer to bet my money when the odds are in my favour.

I locate my room on the ninth floor and find it is modern and a bit tacky but it does have a large Jacuzzi spa bath. I go for a swim in the Olympic sized swimming pool on the roof terrace, where I have a beautiful view of the city below. Then I return to my air conditioned room to read for a while until I ring Marcia. The book I have brought with me is a true story about a bunch of venture capitalists and how they made millions of dollars by investing in internet companies. Among the companies they funded are eBay (still a success of sorts I believe) and the now totally defunct Webvan.

I ring Marcia's cell phone but get no reply. Half an hour later I try again but there is still no answer. The third time I ring the phone is answered by a man who I presume is her husband. I hang up. Something is clearly amiss. I get out my laptop computer and connect it to the room's phone line. Then I dial up onto the internet and send Marcia an email.

'Marcia, are you OK? I can't get you on the phone.'

I check my email an hour later.

'Paul, my husband knows you are here. I can't see you tonight. I'll come to the hotel tomorrow at noon.'

Damn. How has this happened? In the hotel bar I drown my sorrows and retire to bed early.

The next day I read my book, go for a swim and wait for Marcia. I try to leave the hotel to explore outside but after a hundred yards or so I am beaten back by the heat. No one walks in Mississippi in summertime. Everyone drives air conditioned cars.

At noon there is a knock on my door. I rush to open it and am relieved to find it is Marcia. I give her a big hug.

"Are you OK, darling?" I say.

"Yes I'm fine but last night I had a big row with my husband. One of his friends saw us together at the airport and now he is mad."

"What did you tell him?"

"I said you were a friend of my aunt and I was just giving you a lift to your hotel."

"Did he believe you?"

"I don't know but he wouldn't let me go out last night. But I am here now."

"Are you hungry?" I ask.

"Only for you, darling."

Marcia pushes me onto the bed and smothers me with kisses. I was thinking of having something to eat but then pussy is my favourite food.

"Let's get in the Jacuzzi and fuck," I say.

In the afternoon we sleep until Marcia has to go home to ensure she arrives home before her husband becomes suspicious.

"I'll come and see you at the same time tomorrow," she says.

Monday morning arrives and I start packing as I have a 3pm flight back to San Francisco. Marcia arrives at noon as she promised and she is dressed in a short denim wrap-around skirt and a small blue T-shirt. It is clear that she is not wearing a bra.

"I am not wearing any knickers," she teases, lifting her skirt and flashing me a glimpse of her pussy. "I thought that would save time when you fuck me."

It does save time. I don't even take off her trainers. I just give her a quick, dirty fuck on the bed.

I finish packing and check out of the hotel. Marcia drives me to the New Orleans airport.

"I'm gonna miss you, Paul."

"Not as much as I'm gonna miss you, Baby."

At the airport we embrace and I enter the terminal building. San Francisco to New Orleans is a long way to go for two fucks.

Chapter 27: Californication

I have settled in at Buzzsaw. They seem to like me or at least put up with me. I think they view me as lazy, money-oriented but very good. Most of the permanent staff put in free overtime but then they have got stock options and will be millionaires by Christmas. I don't work for nothing. Period. Occasionally they authorise me to do paid overtime but only when they have an urgent requirement.

One evening a week the social secretary for Buzzsaw (there really is one) organises a gathering at one watering hole or another around San Francisco. I usually go along but try to remain sober. It's not easy. After a while I get bored. One Friday night I go out drinking alone. I get a bit merry and decide to locate a strip joint I have heard of called 'Shooters'. I am drinking in a tourist area of San Francisco called Pier 39. By the way it is miles from Pier 38 where I live. I have no idea where 'Shooters' is so I go along to the taxi rank.

"Shooters, yeah, I know it," says the young man driving the taxi. "So you're looking for girls, eh?"

"Yes, I suppose I am," I reply.

"Well, Shooters is OK but it's just a titty bar, you won't see any pussy."

"Oh." I'm not really that bothered - I just want to go somewhere, look at pretty girls and buy them a drink. I'm sad aren't I?

"I could take you to O'Farrell Street."

"What's there?"

"Well, there's a couple of full strip joints, plus I hear the girls will play with you if that's what you like. They're not allowed to sell alcohol but there are bars nearby so you can have a drink first."

"O'Farrell Street it is," I say.

After a couple of drinks in a bar, I approach the cheapest of the strip joints. It is called the New Century. $20 gets me in and I get another $20 in one dollar bills for tipping the strippers. It's 9.30pm and pretty quiet. There's just one girl, who has large false boobs and is not my type at all, stripping on a stage and a few punters sitting around. The record she's dancing to seems very appropriate; it's 'Californication' by the Red Hot Chili Peppers.

I sit at the back and order a sprite. The girl finishes her routine, puts her panties back on, and another dancer comes on the stage. The first girl, still in just her panties, walks straight over to me.

"Would you like a private dance? Sixty dollars," she says, as she strokes the inside of my thigh.

"OK." I don't know what you get here for $60 but I might as well find out. She leads me into a corridor, which has a lot of small rooms leading off it. Heavy curtains make up the door to each of these rooms. In one of the rooms I find out what you get for $60. Not a lot. Much like what you can see on the stage, only close up. I don't fancy her anyway.

"For another sixty dollars you can touch my pussy," she says.

"No thanks." I have already paid her so I return to the stage area. Wow! There are girls everywhere and a lot of punters. It's around 10.30pm now and, from somewhere or other, girls and customers have just materialised. There's still only one girl on stage at a time but other girls tartly dressed (or undressed) wander around asking members of the audience if they want a private dance.

I find out later that 10pm is the time the majority of the girls start work. Mostly they are freelancers who pay the club a fee to work and make their money from tips and private dances.

I sit at the back again to watch for a while when a gorgeous, very dark, black girl sits beside me.

"Come in the back. Twenty dollars. I promise you won't be disappointed."

I've now only got forty dollars left in my wallet. There is an ATM in the club but there are limits as to what I want to spend looking at pussy. Twenty dollars, though, that's a good deal and she is gorgeous.

As she writhes naked on the very small bed in front of me, she plays with my crotch. I am very stiff.

"Can I kiss your pussy?" I ask.

"OK, but it's another twenty dollars," she murmurs.

Without another word I go down on her shaven mound and labia. She tastes as sweet as honey. She is moaning softly. God I could do with a fuck. I think again about the ATM but settle for her phone number. Her name is Patra.

It's October and Marcia tells me that she still hasn't got her green card. She agrees to visit me again - same routine as before but this time she can only spend three nights with me. She's been a bit distant on the phone recently and I can't wait to see her in person.

When she arrives something's not quite the same. She spends a lot of time on her mobile phone and isn't very talkative. Especially about coming to stay with me permanently. She tells me she has no money but dresses expensively (and sexily) and carries a lot of credit cards in her wallet. Gold ones too. She uses my laptop to access her email but she is very secretive over her messages. She's still a good fuck and I am still in love with her but I am suspicious.

I decide to break into her email. I download off the internet and onto my laptop some free software that will invisibly record the keystrokes made on the keyboard. Yes this stuff exists, and the CIA use it too. The next time she accesses her email, her password is recorded. Bingo.

Reading back through her email messages, I soon have the answer. She doesn't have an aunt in Virginia but another boyfriend. I confront her and she reluctantly admits the truth. She loves me (apparently) but she loves the other guy more. He is young, black, in the navy and he has promised to marry her as soon as she is free. Marcia seems to like young, military men. Game over. She flies to Virginia. I am left counting how many fucks I got for flying her to her boyfriend. Fourteen last time, only seven this. Not a bad deal I suppose.

I console myself with Patra. She is expensive at $300 a fuck but she is worth it and I am earning a fortune. Her shaved pussy is exquisite. She lets me fuck her without a condom as long as I don't come inside.

"I'm very fertile," she says.

I can believe it. I am extremely happy as gobs of my spunk spatter onto her very dark almost jet black complexion and her pouting lips covered in bright red lipstick. She has sensibly closed her eyes. She giggles as I hand her a box of tissues.

"You are a naughty boy," she says.

Before our sex sessions I feed Patra on champagne and she brings her own pot to smoke. I am not sure what else she's on but whatever it is I think it costs her a lot of money. She's only 23 and probably ruining her life. But what can I do? If I don't fuck her, someone else will. It's simple economics.

It's after Christmas and the NASDAQ still hasn't recovered. In fact it's got worse. Buzzsaw begin making layoffs but I survive the culls because they still need changes to the marketplace. It still isn't live yet and quite honestly I don't think it ever will be. The Ariba marketplace software is fairly well written but the system isn't flexible enough. We are having to make too many changes to it and Dave and Mike just aren't as good as they think they are. There are holes in the system. Huge holes. No one asks for my opinion and I don't give it. I am making $3000 a week and the meter is still running.

Patra is costing me $600 a week and I am one month from end of contract. It's Friday February 25th and Patra is on her way. She gets the BART (Bay Area Rapid Transport) train over from Oakland, then catches the metro to the Pier 38 stop. I meet her there. We go for a drink, then back to my place where I already have the champagne chilling in the fridge.

Tonight I have decided to come inside her wearing a condom. After some foreplay on the couch in the lounge, she is naked, on her knees in front of me and expertly sucking my dick as I look out of my apartment window and survey the lights twinkling out in the bay. I have a view of Oakland on the other side of the bay and I wonder whereabouts exactly this enchantress lives. Oakland's a rough area. I've been there a couple of times. I know Patra carries a knife - she showed it to me.

I slip on a condom and lead her to the bedroom. I spread her legs apart and, after a bit of cunnilingus, I begin banging her. I am a little rough. I am about five strokes from orgasm when she says, "I need to go to the bathroom."

"OK," I say. Damn. Just five more strokes. I lie on the bed and rest. I like Patra. I wish I could help her but I don't see how. She doesn't love me - she wants my money. It's the economy, stupid. I hear the apartment door slam. I get out of bed and check the bathroom. No Patra. The living room is empty. I check my wallet. Empty. She's taken all the money except for a single $20 note.

She's rolled me for about $600 but she hasn't taken my credit cards. I'm pissed off. I ring her number and leave a message on her answering machine.

"I'm calling the fucking police," I rage. In the end I don't. Half the money she had nearly earned anyway and maybe I was being too rough. I actually feel rather guilty. I think I should have tried harder to help her.

The contract is coming to an end; Buzzsaw don't want to renew and I've had enough. The layoffs are continuing and the marketplace software is due to go live any day now. I hear later that it does go live but is pulled from the site about a month afterwards. "Too many holes in the system and not enough customer interest," I hear on the grapevine.

I am on the plane back to London. I now have twenty thousand pounds in the bank - maybe I'll take a year off and finish writing that book I started ten years ago. Or maybe I'll find another contract. But first things first. I summon the airline stewardess.

"Whisky on the rocks, please. A large one."

Chapter 28: A Sad Story

Back in London I start looking for a new contract. The I.T. (information technology) job market is in ruins. The Internet market has collapsed, the telecommunications market has collapsed. The industry is awash with unemployed I.T. contractors.

Boredom soon begins to get a serious grip on me so I make a radical decision. Since I am unemployed and unattached, I might as well have another holiday in the Far East before continuing with my tedious and unrewarding job search. I book the first cheap flight to Manila that I can find and then relax for a few days at my brother's waiting for my flight.

On the long claustrophobic flight out to Manila I manage to keep my drinking under control. Whoever said "better to travel than to arrive" obviously had never flown long-haul pig-class.

I start to feel better as I exit the airplane and feel the warm blast of Philippine air with its mixture of tempting exotic smells. I search for the airport transfer I have booked and I soon find a gorgeous Filipina attendant holding up my name on a placard. She efficiently shepherds me through the lunch time crowds and towards the waiting minibus. I am very tired from the flight and exchange only a few short pleasantries with the other occupants before slumbering on the way to Angeles.

A few hours later I am relaxing in my deluxe room at the 'Narra Hotel' and am slowly preparing to go out for the evening. The deluxe room is a bit more expensive than the standard but I think the extra money is worth it. I am now forty two years old and my body needs its creature comforts.

After visiting a few bars, I enter the Lollipop bar where, dancing on the stage, is a stunning-looking girl with a bob haircut, small firm breasts and a perfect smile. More importantly she's lithe and moves effortlessly on the stage, occasionally doing the splits to demonstrate her body's flexibility. I am sure she is the 'A' girl at this bar for the moment.

I quickly tell my waitress that I want to buy the girl a drink. The waitress relays my message to the dancer who looks up and over at me, sizes me up instantly and then smiles warmly. I am probably the right age for her. She looks in her early twenties and I look about thirty-five. I am not so old as to be embarrassing nor too young to be too foolish or too demanding. She walks over suggestively in her black thigh high boots and a skimpy skirt covering her panties.

The conversation follows the usual routine. I find out that her name is Raquel and she is 22.

"You're a very good dancer," I tell her.

"Thank you," she says. "Do you mind if I smoke?"

"No, I don't mind," I say. She walks off to fetch her cigarettes but turns to flash a smile at me as she goes. Up close it is apparent that she is wearing quite a lot of makeup and seems surprisingly a little nervous and vulnerable. I am fascinated by her. As she gets her cigarettes from her bag I notice that she takes a large swig of beer from a pint glass by the stage. It is one addict looking at another addict. I decide to bar-fine her if she will come with me. I want to talk to her, amongst other things.

I buy her another drink and order more rum and coke for me.

"Do you want a bar-fine?" I ask.

She is hesitant but then says, "OK. But we have to go now. My boyfriend will come looking for me soon."

"All right, go and change your clothes."

I'll worry about the boyfriend later - right now my priority is to get her off the premises. I pay her bar-fine. Raquel returns having changed into jeans and a T-shirt. She still looks gorgeous.

"Where are you staying?" she asks.

"The Narra," I say.

"I have to bring my things. I have a suitcase."

This is very unusual and I am a bit apprehensive as we venture out into the brightly lit street carrying her suitcase. Raquel is looking around furtively until she pulls me into another bar further down the street.

"I saw my boyfriend. He is a Korean. He is on drugs."

I look out from the bar and see a heavy-looking Korean on the other side of the street. He appears to be in his twenties and he looks mean. Raquel and I stay in the bar, order drinks and allow time to pass. After half an hour, we quickly check outside, hail a trike and make for 'The Narra'. First mission accomplished. The girl is safely at my hotel and I haven't been beaten or worse.

In my hotel room Raquel is still agitated.
"My boyfriend has got me on drugs," she says. "I need a fix." She can't relax. I pour us both rum and coke from the mini bar.
"Can I smoke some crack in your bathroom?" she asks.
"OK I suppose," I reply. This is probably a very bad idea but I know what it's like to be an addict.
"Do you want some, Honey?" she asks.
"No thanks." Alcoholism's bad enough for me and if I got caught with crack here in the Philippines I'd likely get shot. Just having the stuff on this girl is very risky. Where's that rum bottle. I need a fix.

It's been over half an hour and Raquel still hasn't emerged from the bathroom. I do hope she hasn't overdosed. I knock on the door, open it and see her squatting in the corner smoking something. Her eyes are glazed over but she is relaxed and happy.
"Sure you don't want some, Honey?"
"Yeah, I'm sure. Are you OK?"
"I am now. Nearly finished."

I leave her to it and five minutes later she comes out of the bathroom smiling.
"Do you want to see some pictures, Honey?"
"Yeah. Sure."

She opens her suitcase and pulls out some photo albums. She then proceeds to show me photos of her family and her ex-boyfriends. She tells me her story.

A couple of years ago she had two American boyfriends and one was in the army. The army boyfriend wanted to marry her and take her to Korea where he was stationed. The other guy was nicer to her but he was out of the country. The military man proposed and she accepted. When her other boyfriend had found out he pleaded with her to wait until he could come and see her. But 'a bird in the hand' as they say. The marriage was a disaster. In Korea she was mistreated and abused. She had lost the boyfriend she preferred and who loved her. Returning to the Philippines to escape her marriage she took to drink and met a Korean. He wanted to take her to Amsterdam. The Korean had introduced her to drugs a month ago. She was on a spiral down with no way back. Now she wanted to get to Manila to escape the Korean. That's why she had packed her suitcase.

By now she is relaxed and very amorous.

"Kiss my pussy, Honey. I like it."

I oblige her. She's extremely supple and very enthusiastic in bed.

In the morning she says she has to go but she agrees to meet me in the hotel restaurant at noon. Raquel leaves her suitcase in my room. By the time she arrives at noon she is nervous and strung out again. She doesn't want to eat. I take her to my room where I decide to try and help her. I give Raquel five thousand pesos (100 dollars) to get her to Manila with some spending money. She'll probably just spend it on drugs but at least I've given her a fighting chance. She is very relieved as she takes a trike to the main bus station. I don't see her in Angeles again although I can still find her picture in the comfort room of the bar where she used to work. Where are you now my Honey? Most likely dead.

Chapter 29: Bang; Bang; Bang

On my way back to London I am going to stop off in Thailand for a week. I am going to drink heavily and behave terribly.

In Pattaya I stay again in 'The Carlton'. I am a creature of habit and if I find somewhere I like I tend to stick with it.

In the evenings I cruise the bars drinking. It's a strange lifestyle but it suits me. I look back at my life and see the choices I made. I was destined to be where I am. I was never going to have a wife, two point four kids, a family car and a house in the suburbs. I am just far too unstable. I like excitement and risk. Risky places, risky people and risky behaviour.

They say that in life two things are unavoidable. Taxes and death. Well, some taxes are avoidable. I haven't paid any income tax this year because I haven't earned anything. In fact I got a tax rebate from the U.S. government of about three thousand dollars. However, death isn't avoidable. We are all going to die. It is easy to forget this when you are young and healthy but when you are older with health problems or when you have been close to death, it seems very real. For some death can even seem to be a blessed relief.

I am not intending to die yet and when I do die, I want to have lived. I want to have taken risk.

I am walking to my favourite restaurant for lunch when I see a stunning Thai girl outside a short-time bar. She has got the most amazingly pretty face that I have ever seen and immaculately kept, very long, straight black hair, which runs all the way down her back and past her bottom. I enter the bar and buy her a drink. Her English is not very good but when she smiles at me, I just melt.

In stilted conversation I find out she is twenty-two, divorced and has two children. She works so that she can send her children to school. How many times have I heard that story? More often than I can remember. Here education is seen as the way out of misery and poverty. In England education is seen by many young people as something best avoided.

"You want short time?" she asks.

"Hell yes."

She leads me upstairs and into a bedroom. She undresses me, undresses herself and then leads me to a shower room where she washes me and examines my dick for any signs of infection.

Naked she loses a little of her lustre. It is clear that her two children have taken a toll on her body and she has bad stretch marks on her abdomen. But I still melt when I look at that face. Satisfied with the state of my dick she leads me back into the bedroom and sucks on my cock until it is firm.

"How you want fuck me?" she asks as she rolls a condom onto my weapon.

"Dog style," I say. She has a pretty arse and a pretty face so dog style will be best. It doesn't last long. Looking into that pretty face is a huge turn-on and very soon I find myself back in the shower room receiving ablutions from my girl.

"You want long-time?" I ask her. I am rather besotted.

"No. Only short-time. I see my kids."

Perhaps it's just as well. Her English isn't really good enough for us to sustain a relationship. But what a pretty face. Unbelievable.

It is my last night in Thailand and I intend to go out with a bang, or, more accurately, three bangs. I have got just enough hard currency on me to pay for three girls and I am going to spend all of it.

I am wandering around the closed bars in Soi 2 when I find what I am looking for. I enter a bar and see three girls dancing together at one end of the stage. They are laughing and joking with each other and appear to be good friends. I sit in front of them and ask their names. One of them can speak good English.

"Are you friends?" I ask her.

"No, we're cousins," she says. "You like three girls?"

She catches on fast. I pay the bar-fines and the girls get changed into their street clothes. We go bar-hopping and I buy the girls as much alcohol as they want. They are all quite pretty without being stunning. One is much darker in colour than the other two, another of them is very reserved. The third girl is the one who can speak English. She is my translator.

It's fun to take three girls out because they will talk and have fun together and I don't have to make a lot of conversation. I am wondering how it will all work out in bed. We find a bar where we take turns to play pool. The evening is going well. Finally we get back to 'The Carlton' where the girls raid my mini-bar for chocolate and beer (and anything else they can get their hands on). I was expecting this.

Once before I had bar-fined two Thai girls at the same time but it didn't work very well because they spent all evening talking to each other. Even when I was fucking them they were still discussing something or other. Probably chatting about the size of my dick or my performance in bed. It was a bit off-putting. With the three girls it works better. While I fuck one girl, the other two chat while watching my technique. At other times they are so busy playing with each other that they barely notice what's going on in bed next to them. I begin by fucking the dark one as she is the prettiest but after a while I notice a dark stain on the bedspread. She is in menstruation.

I get off of her and climb aboard the more reserved girl. She has drunk a lot of alcohol by now and has lost most of her inhibitions. She quickly brings me to a climax with her thrusting pelvis. Two down, one to go.

"Why am I last?" says the girl with the good English. She is annoyed at being ignored so long.

"I like to save the prettiest till last," I lie. She is very passionate and seems keen on me. We fuck to a climax.

"Can I stay all night?" she asks.

"OK," I say. I certainly don't want all three girls to stay all night. They could end up getting very drunk, trashing the room or robbing me blind.

I send two of the girls home at 2am with a tip. The other one sleeps with me until morning. When she leaves I give her a big tip.

"Will you come and see me tonight?" she asks.

"I'm sorry, Honey. I fly home to England today." She looks heartbroken.

My week of excess is over and I am exhausted. I fly back to London with my hopes high and my head full of memories. All I need to do is find a new job. It is that simple.

Epilogue

I borrowed the shotgun from Glen at lunch time. I told him that I wanted to shoot some rabbits invading my father's allotment. Sometimes Glen is very gullible. I sit in a comfortable chair in the lounge admiring the weapon. Precision made; a work of real beauty. The gun barrel fascinates me. I lick the gun-metal at the end of the barrel. It is cold and tastes slightly acidic. I am surprised to find myself becoming aroused.

I put the gun down and reach for the whisky bottle. It's just like the bad old days. It is 5pm and I have drunk nearly a bottle of whisky in under two hours. Emptying the bottle, I pour a final large slug into the empty tumbler and add an equal measure of cheap lemonade. I think about my debts, my aging skill-set, my aging body, and the bad things I have done in my life. I am living alone; bored, depressed and frightened. The book I have written is a failure - no one will publish it. I can't really face the trip back to reality. Not again. I drink the whisky/lemonade mixture in one large gulp. This is my reality; the euphoria induced by alcohol. Here now, in this room, I have no debts, no failure, no problems at all. Just me, the empty whisky bottle and the shotgun. And we have an appointment together.

Holding the loaded shotgun toward me, I lick the gun-metal again. It tastes good. Reaching down, I cock the trigger on the first barrel. One barrel or two? 'One carnation should be enough.' It's a line from a book I like called 'Sati' (by Christopher Pike). My mind is weaving about happily. I open my mouth and close my lips around both barrels of the gun. It is definitely erotic. With a last surge of resolve I pull hard on the trigger and feel two jolts. My head jolts back momentarily and I feel the recoil of the shotgun in my arms. There's no noise, no pain. I seem to be drifting upwards. I feel fantastic. It's the best moment of my life. I am floating effortlessly and I feel a warm glow all over. Everything seems to be happening in slow motion. Slowly, slowly, I roll over and look down.

Oh my God - there's been a terrible accident! Somebody's shot themselves. Blood is spurting rhythmically from a large hole in the skull. There must still be a pulse. I should call an ambulance.

Quickly. I drift closer to the body and examine the wound. Brain and blood are spattered over a wide area and a chunk of the skull has been blown several feet away by the blast. The blood stops spurting and just oozes from the wound. I think the pulse has stopped.

"When did this happen?" I ask myself. I don't remember hearing a shot. I study what is left of the face. He's a fairly attractive 40 something. No oil painting but still in reasonable physical shape. He reminds me of somebody.

I have a panic attack; my heart's pounding ferociously and I feel nauseous. It's not me! I didn't do it! It's a dream! Call an ambulance. Call the police. Wake up. Wake up. Why can't I wake up? The panic subsides but I still feel sick. It's too late for an ambulance - my body is dead. I am merely a disembodied viewer watching over my own corpse. I have an urge to clean up the mess but all I can do is look at it.

Suddenly the phone rings. I look at the clock on the wall - it is nearly six o'clock. Eventually the answer phone picks up the message.

"Hello brother, it's Robert here. I just wanted you to know I'm missing you. Why don't you come back to London? Ring me back and we'll arrange to meet."

God I feel sick. What have I done?

Time passes. Slowly. In the morning the postman delivers mail. I can see by just looking at the envelopes that there are a lot of bills. And final demands printed in red. A pretty bright red, not like the dark, ugly red of the congealing blood caked around the stiffening corpse in the lounge. I examine the corpse again. I used to live there. It used to be my home. Two flies are buzzing around the lifeless body. One alights on some brain matter and begins feeding. I want to swish them away. I see the flies mating excitedly and watch as the female lays her eggs in some exposed flesh. My old home will soon be home to new occupants.

Days pass. More messages are left on the answer phone. Finally, my father leaves a frantic message that he's coming over. The maggots are well infested in the carcass by now and the face is unrecognisable. The smell of decay is overpowering. The body is bloated and yellow. Effortlessly I float outside and wait. An hour later my father arrives. He knocks on the door, then looks in his pocket for his spare key to my house. I want my body to be found but not like this, not by him. I shout at him.

"Call the police! Call the fucking police!" Please Daddy. "Call the fucking police." The tears are streaming from my eyes. He opens the door and recoils from the stench. He knows what he is going to find, I can see it written in his face.

"Call the fucking police!" I shout again. Too late. He finds the body, sees the maggots, the blood, the endgame. He's crying. My old father is crying like a baby. I am crying. What have I done? He recovers, and fighting back the tears he does what I now cannot do. He calls the police.

At the funeral there's a big turnout. Most of my family are there; cousins, aunts, uncles. Glen is there with his wife Elaine and their two children. Glen looks so sad. He must feel bad about lending me the shotgun. As the coffin is brought in and the service proceeds I see my dad is crying again. My mum is weeping too - she looks as though she has been crying for days. My little brother Robert is watery-eyed and even my older brother James looks miserable.

"I am OK," I want to tell them.

At the end of the service the mourners disperse and I am left alone in the chapel. A small white light has been following me for the last few days but it frightens me and I avoid it. I visit my old house. Empty. I visit my brothers, my parents. I visit Glen. Their lives continue but now they are carrying a bit more sorrow. Some are carrying a huge burden of sorrow for my wasted life.

The light is bigger and brighter now and more persistent. I visit the chapel where I was cremated and see the flowers left for me aging and withered. The light pursues me with a vengeance. I retreat to my old house. A 'For Sale' sign stands outside - the mortgage company have foreclosed and want their money back. The bills are piled high from creditors who will not now ever be paid. My family will have to pay for my cremation.

I look down at the scene of my crime. Cleansed of most of the evidence it's hard to believe I did what I did. The light comes into the room and moves closer. It's huge now and fills the room. As I look at it, it is suddenly clear. The light isn't in the room - the room is in the light. The house is in the light. The light is vast, unending, overwhelming and beneficent. Beautiful beyond description and full of love. Now I see. Everything is in the light. No, no -

everything is the light and the light is truth and love. With that thought ringing in my head I begin to lose consciousness, feeling just a momentary flickering of the light as it welcomes me home. Vast and unending though it is, it still finds time to acknowledge the passing of one of its many billions of children.

I have moved from consciousness to unconsciousness, from separation to unity, from the many to the one. It's over. Will I get a chance at reincarnation or is one incarnation enough? Only the one knows.

I wake up in a cold sweat. I am wet through and shaking. It's a recurring nightmare. I look at the whisky bottle I keep by my bedside. It's unopened. I relax a little - I have another precious day of life.

Everyday I take out the shotgun.
Everyday I taste the gun-metal.
Everyday I make a decision.
Everyday I choose life.
Choose life.
And remember, there is a God; there must be.

MY FINAL JOURNEY WITH ALCOHOLISM

(A Short Guide to Addiction & Redemption)

Paul Pisces

Copyright © Paul Pisces 2023

All rights reserved. No part of this publication may be reproduced, stored in a retrieval system, or transmitted in any form or by any means, electronic, mechanical, photocopy, recording or otherwise, without prior written permission of the copyright owner. Nor can it be circulated in any form of binding or cover other than that in which it is published and without similar condition including this condition being imposed on a subsequent purchaser.

DISCLAIMER

Stopping an addiction is potentially dangerous because of withdrawal. If you are in doubt, please discuss your addiction with your doctor before you stop your addictive behavior. This is especially true if you are on medication, have other medical conditions or if you are a chronic addict.

MY FINAL JOURNEY WITH ALCOHOLISM
by Paul Pisces

Prologue:
Chapter 1: Alcoholic!
Chapter 2: The Morning After
Chapter 3: Zurich, Switzerland
Chapter 4: Trouble at the Mill
Chapter 5: Langstrasse, Zürich
Chapter 6: Novo Nordisk
Chapter 7: Reinsurance from Hell
Chapter 8: Mental Hospital or Suicide?
Chapter 9: Mercy Dash
Chapter 10: Rehab
Chapter 11: Miracle
Chapter 12: Sika Relapse!
Chapter 13: Sobriety in the Long Term
Chapter 14: Final Thoughts
Epilogue

MY FINAL JOURNEY WITH ALCOHOLISM
by Paul Pisces

Prologue

My early journey with alcoholism is detailed in my first book "Desperately Seeking Sex & Sobriety". In that book I descend into chronic alcoholism during my twenties and thirties and then regain some control in my early forties.

Unfortunately, this situation does not last and like many alcoholics I am doomed to fall further before hitting a rock bottom.

This new descent involves mental hospitals, rehab, and long suicidal periods.

However, I am one of the lucky ones.

I am still alive.

Chapter 1: Alcoholic!

After my experiences in the dot com boom and bust in San Francisco, (see "Desperately Seeking Sex & Sobriety") I return to London to consider my options.

I now have some savings and I am currently just about managing my alcoholism.

I am 42 and living again with my brother in Hammersmith (West London) and looking for a new job.

After the dot com bust in 2001, the whole I.T. job market has taken a catastrophic hit. There are few jobs and many applicants.

I sit about depressed and drinking on and off. I know I am an alcoholic – I have known this since I was 30 – but I don't want to stop. Drinking is my life. Without any alcohol I just don't know how I would exist. I don't know how I would fill my time, fill the day.

It is noon on Wednesday the 6th of February 2002. To ease the depression and boredom of my now 42-year-old body, I am going to take you on a crash course of alcoholism.

Right now, I am stone cold sober, but I am going to open and drink a bottle of white rum and describe the effects on my mind and body. Perhaps more honestly, it is just a good excuse for me to get drunk.

A bottle of rum is more than I should drink in a binge but with my metabolism, half a bottle would be just too easy. It wouldn't hurt enough. I hope this is the last time I drink a whole bottle in one sitting, but it may not be. (It wasn't.)

Please do not try this at home, especially if you do not know what you are doing. A bottle of spirits can kill an inexperienced drinker.

Now outside it is sunny. Inside I am calm, but I am feeling a bit depressed. I could certainly use a drink.

The first taste is good – for an alcoholic it is just like meeting an old friend. I drink a half and half mixture of rum and coke, and the alcohol is sharp against the palate.

To occupy myself during the day, I normally find a book to read. I am reading a lot of autobiographies currently. I like this genre, particularly if the author is honest and has had an unusual lifestyle.

I have read a couple by city traders, one by a guy with mental health problems, one by a bouncer, and several others. They have almost all been good, some have been excellent.

The big problems I have at the moment are that the alcohol is killing me and I'm getting a bit long in the tooth to work in I.T. – that doesn't leave a lot, does it? And the truth is that after working in San Francisco during the dot com boom, working anywhere else is a bit tame by comparison. It's like playing in the World Cup at football (soccer) and then being asked to play for a third division side – difficult to get motivated.

Thirty minutes have passed, and I have now consumed one fifth of the bottle. No real effect yet, although I do feel slightly looser. It only gets interesting after half a bottle. The recovery tomorrow will be much less fun.

I could drink this bottle much more quickly, but I want to take my time over it and write this story. The plan is to consume the bottle over the course of the afternoon and evening (maybe 7 or 8 hours). When the bottle is empty, I will go to bed and sleep. I will almost certainly sleep well with all the alcohol inside me.

Prior to sleeping I expect to be very happy, almost euphoric. My brother is out on a training course today, so I am alone, but I do have a couple of housekeeping tasks to take care of.

It's 1pm and a third of the bottle is gone. I feel loose and uninhibited – it's nice. I am relaxed and unworried about anything. I am glad to be writing. Although I am on my own in the house, I feel sociable. I'd like someone to talk to, but I don't need anyone.

I am happy on my own doing a few household chores (washing, washing-up) and watching the TV (Spin City, Cheers). American television shows seem to dominate British television during the afternoon. Later I might watch "Oprah", or I might continue reading Andy McNab's autobiography "Immediate Action" about his life in the SAS.

Life feels good but I know it is illusory – dark storm clouds are gathering on my horizon. My life is not stable or secure. I know where I want to be, but it is not in my control. I feel like a pawn on a chessboard or a piece of flotsam in a fast-moving river. My future is controlled by others.

How do I control my fear? There are many elements. The most important is God. The most interesting question of all questions (perhaps it is the only real question) is "Is there a God or not?" So much of life rests on this question that the impact of how you answer it is incalculable.

It's still only 1:30pm and I've nearly drunk half the bottle of rum. I am starting to feel a little bit tired – not very tired but I could sleep. Heavy drinking in an alcoholic causes two conditions: sick and tired. I don't feel sick today, although I have done many times in the past, but I do feel tired.

The alcohol is depressing my motor functions and my brain functions causing them to shut down. Sleep looks attractive. Is there anything attractive about the way I feel? No, not really. If I was younger, I would probably be less tired and more sociable.

Hey, it's lunch time - I'll have something to eat because I have got to pace myself. I am trying to perform an experiment. I heat a spaghetti Bolognese in the microwave and eat in front of the telly watching snooker. It's 2pm and I'm feeling a bit depressed again. I'm in a melancholy state - not yet happy from the alcohol and not stone cold sober. I am an addict waiting for the high to kick in. My mental weakness is now apparent, and I feel empty. The options are simple: go to bed and sleep till I feel better or drink more until the alcohol euphoria takes over.

If I were sensible, I'd go to bed. I've consumed half a bottle of rum in two hours and that should be more than enough for me. But this is an experiment so it's onwards and upwards. I am doing myself definite damage, but this may be the last time and at least it is documented.

I don't want to drink anymore alcohol. I could easily pour the remaining half bottle away. It is very good that I feel this way - it means that I have some control over my addiction. My overall feeling currently is just tired. I'd still like to sleep. The alcohol is depressing all my body's systems, and they want to switch off. This is partly due to old age - my body is weaker and needs more rest.

Alcohol is a potent depressant drug and in the absence of stimulation the tendency is to sleep. Everything is starting to switch off now and the prospect of sleep is very real.

By 4pm I am still tired and sleepy with just over half the bottle gone. But this is the low point and soon the alcohol will begin to lift me and make me feel euphoric. The interesting thing though is that it's not worth a candle and I'd rather be sober and sharp. My relationship with alcohol has changed as I've got older, and my metabolism is less able to handle it. Whereas before alcohol would make me feel happy and confident, now it makes me sick and tired. It's the difference between drinking in your twenties and drinking in your thirties and forties. The damage to the body catches up to you and your metabolism begins to creak. I will hit my euphoric high later, but it will be at a severe physical cost as I will discover tomorrow.

Alcohol is a drug. Alcoholism is an addiction. There are four significant facts about alcohol addiction:

1) The drug is legal (if you are old enough).

2) The drug is relatively cheap.

3) The drug is readily available.

4) The drug is socially acceptable.

If I was an addict of any other drug I would by now almost certainly be either on the street, in prison or dead. Drugs rob us of our intellect and our morals. Eventually they will rob us of our health, our freedom and even our sanity. Why does anyone take a recreational drug? Well, I think it's a combination of excitement and escape. But what is it that we are trying to escape from? What is it in society that drives our need to escape? Modern society is very stressful. The pressures on the population are intense and growing. There is little security and there is little support for those who fall by the wayside. Even in the so-called free society of the west, there is little real freedom.

We have exchanged our individual freedom for a culture of corporate slavery in a hierarchy that is accountable to no one except faceless shareholders. The system is called capitalism. Now unfettered due to the collapse of the communist threat, the capitalistic greed is running rampant and those in power use their positions to pressurise those beneath them for the maximum benefit of themselves.

In many ways this is astonishing. The purpose of leadership should be to sacrifice oneself for the benefit of those being led but capitalism seems to operate to the contrary. To be fair communism is no better and probably worse because it is a dictatorship but, in a democracy, we should expect more from our leaders.

We spend about eight hours asleep, and this is our freedom - our time with God. We spend about eight hours at work. No freedom here for most just rules and regulations imposed in large part by fools and bullies. This leaves a maximum of eight hours to administrate our lives: pay bills, commute to work, do housework and generally survive with maybe only two or three hours of real 'free' time.

I believe much of the problem lies at work. We need to move away from capitalism and towards a more cooperative society. Capitalism plays to greed. It plays to short term views. It plays to, if not outright dishonesty, to something less than the truth. To less than excellence.

"And what is good, Phaedrus, and what is not good. Need we ask anyone to tell us these things?" (from 'Zen and the Art of Motorcycle Maintenance' by Robert M. Pirsig)

We all know what is good, we all know what is excellent. Why don't we try harder to achieve it for ourselves and for others.

It's 5-30pm and I have slowed my drinking. I am inebriated. Not drunk but chilled out. I've now drunk two thirds of the bottle. The sleepiness has gone, and I am beginning to feel cheerful, optimistic, euphoric and powerful. The nicest thing about getting inebriated and euphoric is the optimism. Now I can view my future in a much more positive light. What do I know?

To the positive:

1) I am reasonably bright.

2) I am well educated.

3) I still have an I.T. career.

To the negative:

1) I am getting old.

2) I am an alcoholic.

3) I am bored working with computers.

Alcohol moves my perspective to the positive, but it is a fool's gold because to make the most of the positives above, I need to be stone cold sober.

Getting drunk or inebriated for me is a largely pleasant process. I am a happy drunk. I am not aggressive or violent. I am relaxed and cheerful. Also, I am happy to drink at home, alone. When I was younger, I would prefer to drink in a pub or club and in company. While drinking I would enjoy playing pool or dancing depending on the venue.

6pm has arrived. There is a fifth of a bottle left, which is very little from an alcoholic's point of view. I am drunk and I will pay for my high tomorrow when I begin to sober up. Getting up there is easy no matter what drug you choose to use. Alcohol, amphetamine, coke, e, heroin, crack, or hash. You can get up there with anything, but can you come back down?

It's the down that hurts.

It's 7pm and I am very drunk. It feels good but there are no real advantages at all. I am again feeling very tired, and I just want to sleep and pretend that if only I were more sociable, I could find a woman who'd like to spend time with me. Deep within me I know that this is rubbish.

The bottle is empty and now I am in a bad state. There is nothing pleasant to say about my descent to a state of manic euphoria. I am desperately tired.

"Fuck you. What do you know? Nothing. I am the way, the truth and the light and I am dying. Will you fight to save me? I don't think so. The horsemen of the apocalypse are on their way and there is little to stop them. I have had enough in all respects. I have drunk enough; I have thought enough, and I have lived enough."

I stagger upstairs to bed and collapse.

Chapter 2: The Morning After

I wake up early at 6am. I feel bad. In the old days I would be reaching for the whisky, vodka, or rum bottle for the first drink of the day. Instead, I reach for the fizzy water bottle. Fluids are important for recovery, especially water. Loads of it. After a pint of water, I decide to have a cup of coffee. I don't have the shakes because I haven't been on alcohol for a long enough continuous period.

I don't have a hangover (headache, nausea) because alcoholics don't often get these, but I do feel very agitated and unable to relax. I don't remember last night very well. I don't remember going to bed but I woke up in bed so I must have, probably around 7-30pm. Very early for me but I was so tired. I do remember being tired last night. Very tired indeed.

Although I don't have a headache as such, I do crave peace and quiet. I have turned the telly on but with the sound down. I could work today if I had to, but it would be a struggle. I couldn't do anything complicated because my concentration is bad. I am not at all focused. Fortunately, all I've got to do today is recover. Slowly.

I've read the last page of what I wrote last night, and I was obviously babbling. Mania had set in. Mania is a problem with hardened alcoholics.

One cup of coffee down, so I'll go and make another. Two cups of coffee, a poop and plenty of fizzy water. That's the recipe for today.

Today's big news is of a trader in America with an Irish bank who has 'lost' $750 million dollars in currency speculation. A bit like Nick Leeson and Barings Bank. I've read Nick Leeson's autobiography 'Rogue Trader' and it was very good as I remember. No sex though. No one mentions sex in autobiographies. Except me. I've ordered the comedian Jim Davidson's first autobiography 'The Full Monty' from Amazon.com and I should get it in one or two days' time. I wonder if that will have sex in it. (It didn't.)

The trader in America is of interest to me because I follow the markets, especially since the dot com crash while I was in San Francisco. It appears to me that the markets are still highly overpriced and liable to collapse. The entire capitalist system is being destroyed by greed and incompetence but that's only my opinion - I could be wrong. In fact, I hope I am wrong because if the system collapses, no one will want my computer skills, no one will want me. A bit like the current situation really. OK. I hope the system does collapse then.

I do need quiet. Quiet is important because I am jumpy. My nerves are bad. Even when I am sober, I am an anxious kind of guy. I am always seeking security in terms of financial security and physical security. It's alcohol that gives me a release from the anxiety. Perhaps that's why I have been dependent on it for so long.

After this second cup of coffee, I'll have a poop and then I'll check my email. I'll also check the lottery ticket that I bought yesterday when I was out buying the bottle of rum.

An important tip for recovering alcoholics is not to keep alcohol in the home. If I have alcohol here, I usually drink it. I can overrule this urge but not normally for very long. If it's there I am going to drink it.

The coffee has put some caffeine in my blood stream and that has precipitated my bowels to begin to move. In the toilet my stool is good and reasonably firm. This is a good sign. A hardened alcoholic tends to have sloppy stools or diarrhoea because of the digestive problems alcohol causes.

I am having trouble concentrating. Ideas are coming thick and fast, and I want to do several things at once. This again is normal during recovery. I make lists. The best thing to do is make lists and come back to the tasks later if you can. The other important thing is to try and relax. Find some quiet, drink water, make lists and relax. You'll feel better eventually.

I check my lottery ticket. No win for me. That's another pound down the drain. Next on my list is to check my email. That will take me a while. I am having another cup of coffee but decaffeinated this time. I like the warm fluid, but I don't need any more caffeine in my system. My body is still racing due to the alcohol withdrawal, and I expect that my heart rate and blood pressure are well above normal. I am sweating lightly too. No shakes though.

The worst thing about today is the feeling of not being quite right. Not ill but not well. A feeling of being out of control. I know it's due to the alcohol withdrawal, but it still feels very uncomfortable. The quick way to cure this is to drink alcohol. The sensible way to cure this is to drink water and wait.

By 8am I am getting occasional bursts of lucidity. They don't last long. I am drinking a lot of water and urinating a lot. This allows the body to eliminate the byproducts of alcohol poisoning as quickly as possible. I am calm but my mind is still racing, which continues to make it difficult to concentrate.

Long term alcohol dependence causes many problems such as vitamin loss, poor digestion, physical shaking, and a dry skin, which can lead to eczema and psoriasis. This is in addition to the well-known cirrhosis of the liver. All the cells of the body come under assault and that's why long-term alcoholics look so ill. They are very ill.

It is now noon, so it has been twenty-four hours since I opened the bottle of rum. I have just eaten an early lunch consisting of cheese, ham, tomato, and bread. It is good to eat. I still feel restless, but things are improving, I think. I may not fully recover until tomorrow. You wouldn't be able to tell that anything was wrong with me by looking at me. It's all inside. It's all chemical imbalance in the brain. My brain is working too fast, and I can't relax. I can't focus.

By the evening I am feeling better. Relaxed and calm. My concentration is returning. I spend the evening watching television and eating a takeaway curry. I go to bed early and sleep. Tomorrow I will feel better.

Chapter 3: Zurich, Switzerland

Since I can't find a job in London, I decide to get creative and start to apply for jobs in Europe advertised on the internet. And unbelievably, after a few weeks, I get lucky.

There's a company in Zurich, Switzerland who are interested in my cv and my experience in San Francisco. Holcim are a huge international cement company, but they are currently running a project using the Ariba software I worked on in San Francisco. I do a webcam interview and I am then invited to Zurich for a day of face-to-face interviews. Surprisingly, it all goes well!

I'm offered the job and receive a contract a few days later. With no other offers on the table, I sign on the dotted line and jet off to begin my new life in Switzerland in September 2002.

I rent an apartment and get all my belongings and furniture shipped over from storage in England. Everything is ready for my new life and I am happy to report that Zurich has a small red light district that will probably keep me amused in the evenings.

The two major downsides are that I don't speak German, which is the main language in Zurich, and I know absolutely no-one in the city. It is a lonely start.

Chapter 4: Trouble at the Mill

I start the new job full of hope and optimism but quite soon I begin to feel uneasy. There is a lot of office politics going on here and the whole project is quite disorganised. Nobody is very helpful, and the overall atmosphere appears to indicate that it is every man for himself.

There are also some management consultants from McKinsey here who seem to be tasked with finding out whether this project will ever succeed and make a return on investment. This is what you call "Trouble at the Mill!"

After 3 months it is clear to me that this project is doomed. The costs are out of control and there is no discernible leadership. Management continues to tell everyone that all is well but I am sure that the reality is that the McKinsey consultants have told the senior management to pull the plug.

And that is exactly what happens – I am made redundant with a small payoff and the assurance that Holcim will pay half my removal costs if I decide to return to England.

Meanwhile I embark on another major job search this time in a foreign land. My drinking picks up and for some stress relief I set off for Zurich's red-light district in Langstrasse.

Chapter 5: Langstrasse, Zürich

By this time my typical weekend begins promptly at 5pm on a Friday afternoon. Usually, I and my mainly married colleagues will walk the couple of hundred yards to a bar near the train station which loosely describes itself as a "British Pub". This means the décor and furniture are in poor condition and the beer is warm. They used to have a Filipina working there who could speak English, but she left.

It's not so bad and very convenient for a quick pint or two after work. As I drink, I pull out my packet of continental menthol cigarettes and light up. I only smoke when I drink – in fact I try and keep all my vices together in the hope that they will only count as one sin in total come the final reckoning. I am in many respects a bad man.

I spend an hour with my work mates becoming slowly more and more frustrated at the requirement for me to retain at least a modicum of respectability. Just before 6pm I run for the 6.01 train to the city centre and my transformation from almost respectable employee to crazy alcoholic is nearly complete.

On the train I break out my hip flask and take quiet nips of vodka. I begin to relax after the exacting trials and tribulation of the so recently expired week of work. At the main train station, it is a quick transfer to the bus and a 10-minute ride to the heart of the red-light zone.

My first stop is a Thai style bar, and my usual hostess Nan brings me a glass of dry white Chardonnay as I light up another cigarette. "Drink for me?" Nan asks and I nod almost imperceptibly.

Nan's a cute looking girl and she doesn't look her 30 years. She is slim and dresses in a revealing short skirt and skimpy top. She has a small son and no husband, but I've never been able to tempt her to meet me outside the bar worse luck.

After two more drinks I tip Nan unnecessarily and walk to the main drag of the strip. I have a drink in a few more bars and chat to some girls I know. Almost everyone knows me around here. At work a woman once mentioned that she'd read in the paper that there were 2000 prostitutes in this city. "2000?" I said, "I must know all of them...". Even she thought that was funny.

Most of the freelancers working the bars are African, Brazilian, or Cuban with a sprinkling of Russians and other east Europeans. The Thais are mainly in the erotic clubs and massage parlours which I rarely visit as it is too controlled (and expensive) for my taste.

In one of the bars suddenly Claudia wanders in and immediately makes a beeline for me. "Hey Paul, do you want to buy me a drink?" she coos. "OK," I reply, and she slides in next to me at the bar and begins stroking my thigh.

Claudia is 28, good-looking, African, English speaking, no kids. She has several piercings and I've been with her several times before. "Do you want to come with me short time or I'll stay with you tonight if you like?" She flutters her eyelids mockingly. "OK, short time," I say.

We walk to her small one-room apartment and do the business. It costs me around £100 for an hour. (This is an expensive city.) I emerge from the apartment block into the rain and make my way to my favourite bar. This bar has a band every night and a quiet Thai restaurant/bar attached which is good for chatting once you have selected your potential mate for the night.

I wander through the bar and say hello to several girls and a few of the guys I recognise. I am looking for Nina but, in the end, it is Nina who finds me. In French she exclaims "Paul, where have you been? I've been looking everywhere for you." I smile, escort her to the small, quiet bar and buy a bottle of dry white wine for the two of us.

My O-level French is not very good, but it is good enough for our purposes. "Paul, I want to stay with you tonight. Tomorrow, I must go back to Paris. OK?" I nod. I like Nina. She's also 28, African, French speaking, big smile, and warm personality. She has one kid in Africa and a caesarean.

She's not the cutest girl on the game here but she's has got a nice ass. She is also very friendly, good fun and I trust her enough to have her in my home. I trust Claudia too as it happens but as it turns out tonight is Nina's night. We have something to eat and then get a taxi back to my apartment.

In the morning I drink a bottle of white wine while Nina does a pretty good job of cleaning my apartment. After lunch we retire to the bedroom for an hour. Later we shower together, dry ourselves and get dressed. I give her £400 and then walk her to the train station to buy her a train ticket back to the city.

"A la prochaine fois!" she says as she kisses me. "Yes, see you next time, honey," I reply. She gets aboard the train and waves at me until she's out of sight. I like Nina, she's sweet. They are all sweet – well nearly all.

I spend the rest of Saturday afternoon drinking wine and doing chores until I fall asleep sozzled and content. I have bust my weekend budget of £500 so next weekend I'll have to cut back a bit. Yeah, next weekend...

Sunday is my day of rest. No women, no cigarettes, and no booze. Just a very bad hangover, plenty of bottled water and plenty of sleep. With luck I'll just about be fit for work tomorrow morning.

You might think that this lifestyle is a bit risky. I would say that my lifestyle and that of the girls around me is riskier than most but nowhere near as risky as most people would probably imagine.

You might also think that it is impossible to love a prostitute but that's not true either. I love (in my own way) all the women I associate with. They are different, daring, unusual, sexy, and alluring. They are in addition a surprisingly nice bunch of people.

Prostitution isn't well understood (or well regarded) in the UK. It's generally thought of as a seedy, dirty world populated by drug addicts, pimps, pushers, traffickers, criminals, and sad people (like me).

Now, no doubt all these types of individuals exist in the sex industry here (& elsewhere) but this is largely due to the illegal nature of the trade and the lack, therefore, of any regulation except the prosecution of all and sundry (weather permitting).

I have a great deal of experience of prostitutes. I am 43 and over the last 10 years I have paid for sex with women in the UK, USA, Holland, Switzerland, the Philippines, and Thailand.

I have had good (mostly) and bad experiences. I regard myself as a professional John. Being a professional John, however, doesn't pay well. Sebastian Horsley says in his article "The Brothel Creeper" (Why I've slept with 1000 women) that it cost him £100,000. I've spent a similar amount on only 500 women so he must either be cheap or a better negotiator.

Why do I go to prostitutes? Well, I don't want a traditional girlfriend and I don't want to do one-night stands. Plus, if I pay, I get who I want (within reason) no strings attached.

Prostitution is not all sleaze, pimps, and drugs. It is women's business, and it can be classy and expensive. The double-standard employed by government whereby it appears sex can be packaged and used to sell almost anything for a profit by anyone except women themselves for their own well-being.

Society at large should stop victimising sex workers (and Johns) who are engaging in natural human activity and press for the decriminalisation of prostitution across the world.

Chapter 6: Novo Nordisk

Miracles often come when least expected and this one is no exception. A pharmaceutical company called Novo Nordisk is interested in my cv and has asked me to come in for an interview.

Novo Nordisk is the world's biggest manufacturer of insulin and is another large international enterprise. It is a Danish company, but their European office is in Oerlikon near Zurich.

I saunter down to Oerlikon a bit earlier than necessary and decide to get a haircut before going on to the interview. I am wearing my best suit and am well-turned out and sober!

After the haircut, I present myself at the Novo Nordisk offices and am ushered into an interview with the I.T. director. It goes well and they don't need me to speak German.

I am sent a contract and sign my life away again. This job works a bit better than the previous one, but it is still very stressful and difficult.

The system I am looking after is proprietary and requires a lot of research to keep it up and running. We also again have consultants running around interfering and trying to undermine my position. But such is life in a big I.T. department.

After 5 years of this, my boss the I.T. director is promoted and goes off to run the country office in Turkey. One of the consultants is recruited into his old position. This is not good news for me, and I start looking for a new job.

Chapter 7: Re-insurance from Hell

After a couple of months, I find a new job at a re-insurance company based in offices at Zurich Lake. It's a very nice location but the project is not going so well. I.T. is full of troubled projects and I sometimes wonder how the world keeps functioning amid all the I.T. disasters out there.

After 5 years I was desperate to get out of Novo Nordisk, but this move rapidly becomes an "out of the frying pan into the fire" scenario.

They are basically doing it ALL wrong. They have picked the wrong system, are using it in the wrong way, and have the wrong setup. They are even trying to solve the wrong problem.

"Why did you join then!?" I hear you shouting at me. Well, when you join you don't have all the information. You must take a lot on trust. I did my due diligence, but it wasn't enough. You live and learn, and this is a hard lesson.

I try and tough it out for a few months but in the end, I am just waiting for the project to collapse. If it collapses soon, I may be able to help them do it right next time. But the stress is unbelievable, and my alcohol intake is growing.

My mental health is also suffering so I finally must make a big decision. I resign.

When I walk out of that office by the lake for the last time it is a great relief. But now I have no job, a limited income, and too much time on my hands.

Chapter 8: Mental Hospital or Suicide?

By my calculations, I would say that in my career 1 in 3 bosses have been adequate and 1 in 3 jobs I have held have been survivable. This is not very good odds. Most bosses and most jobs in I.T. are just terrible. And the ones that are not terrible are normally very stressful.

I have been on the brink of breakdown or burn-out many times. The alcoholism has not helped but I don't think it is the primary driver. The stress and the alcoholism feed on each other and create a downward spiral. It is this downward spiral I am now on.

After months on unemployment benefit, I am veering between alcoholic periods and periods of relative sobriety. I even manage to go to a few interviews, but my confidence is at a low ebb.

Eventually, I give up the pretence of normality and give in to full time alcoholism.

It is not a good move as I begin to feel more and more suicidal. I visit the train station often and watch the high-speed trains go by. I find myself on the roofs of tall buildings considering the consequences of the fast way down.

This is getting dangerous. I need to get to a safe place. I call the emergency services and ask for an ambulance. When they arrive, I tell them I am suicidal, and they take me to a mental hospital.

The mental hospital is not fun. No booze. Nothing to do. No-one to talk to. I am bored out of my mind but after a couple of days, I do start to come out of withdrawal and sober up.

As soon as I sober up and begin to feel better, I want to leave but I am locked in and trapped. To pass the time I read every English book they have in their small library.

After a week inside I get a review of my case. I am now pretty much recovered. And no longer suicidal. They agree to let me out.

Walking out into the fresh air is just what I need. Unfortunately, the other thing I think I need is a drink and I make a beeline for my favourite bar. This doesn't work out well…

Chapter 9: Mercy Dash

A few weeks later and I am again drinking all day long and feeling suicidal. All I do is drink, watch porn and sleep. It is a terrible existence and I want to end it all. I really want to stop this misery and end it.

I go to the top of a high building near my apartment and get over the balcony rails on the tenth floor. I think about it. Then I give up and climb back to safety. I haven't got what it takes to kill myself. Not yet.

But I do need to do something. If I call the emergency services again, they will take me back to the mental hospital and God knows how long I'll be in there. I need help. Urgent help.

I go back to my flat, pick up the telephone and call my 76-year-old dad.

"Dad, I'm suicidal", I say. "I don't know what to do."

"Can you fly home, Son?", he asks.

"No, Dad. I can't make it. I am too unstable."

"OK, Son. Give me one hour and I'll call you back."

True to his word, an hour later the phone rings. He explains the plan. My two brothers will rent a car and drive all the way from London to Zurich to pick me up. They will then take me to the Priory in Chelmsford. The Priory is a mental hospital and rehab centre and Chelmsford is a town just outside London.

It will take them twelve hours to get to me. That means I have at least twelve more hours of drinking time.

Chapter 10: Rehab

I arrive at the Priory late in the evening of the 3rd of March 2009 and I am in terrible shape. I didn't get enough alcohol on the drive back to England and am now in serious withdrawal. I am shaking and having bad mental health problems.

After a quick assessment by a doctor, the Priory dispense sedatives and show me to my room. As soon as I am alone, I look for suitable suicide hanging points. I don't find any good ones. I try and sleep without much success.

The following morning at a group therapy discussion I meet my fellow inmates and the Addiction Therapy Program (ATP) is explained to me.

I am supposed to stay here for 28 days and during that time I am allowed little contact with the outside world. All phones are taken away and we are secluded in our own little world of alcoholism and drug addiction.

There is lots of group therapy during the day and in the evenings, we are escorted to AA (Alcoholics Anonymous) or NA (Narcotics Anonymous) meetings in the local area. There is also a big focus on the 12 steps of Alcoholics Anonymous during the group therapy.

On reflection, I like the 12 steps of AA. In fact, I like everything about AA except the part where I must stop drinking!

After a few days the shaking stops and I get used to the new environment. It is much better than the mental hospital in Zurich and at least everyone speaks English. I even start to enjoy myself on occasion.

The other inmates I am with are a friendly bunch and my three best friends are the owner of an upmarket hairdressers (who has alcohol and coke addictions), an older business owner with a long-term serious alcohol problem and a young chef with a chronic vodka addiction.

My three friends all seem to be here to try and save their relationships, but I know that I am here to try and save my life. We all stick together at group therapy and at mealtimes. I don't think I could survive here without these guys.

The staff all tell me I shouldn't project into the future but then they aren't sitting in the loony bin with their lives going up in smoke halfway across Europe. The future, even if I can get sober, is very, very bleak.

The days pass and I begin to get some clarity, but I still can't see how I can possibly rescue my life from this dismal point.

Halfway through the program everyone celebrates my 50th birthday on March 18th. I get two cakes: one from the ATP team and one from the hospital itself. I overdose on sucrose, but this is allowed.

My family continue to be very supportive but don't want me to go back to Zurich. Privately I now think I must go back – Zurich is where my home is, but I keep this to myself.

Chapter 11: Miracle

I have given my younger brother my email address and password because I am not allowed to have any internet access. The day after my birthday he comes to see me and says, "You've received an interesting email from a company called Sika – they have offered you a job!"

Oh my God! Sika is a company I interviewed with months ago before my last desperate downward spiral. I need to contact them, but no one will help me. My family and the staff all want me to stay in England. They say I should concentrate on the program and not worry about a job in Zurich.

They are crazy! This is a miracle! I must accept this job and go back. It is my only lifeline.

When the chips are down, there is always a way. As I said before the Priory is a mental hospital as well as a rehab centre and some of the other patients are allowed phones.

I approach one of the patients and ask to borrow his smartphone. He is happy to help. Using this phone, I access my email and get the phone number of Sika's HR department.

I then collect as many one-pound coins as I can from my friends and head to the one public phone in the hospital. I ring the number and explain to the HR department that I'd love to accept the position, but could I start on the 1st May because I am currently on holiday in England.

They are happy to postpone my joining for a month and they say they will send the contract to my Zurich address for me to sign.

Mission accomplished!

I have one last chance at redemption. I hope I don't blow it!

Chapter 12: Sika Relapse!

The twenty-eight days are up and there is a small celebration at my leaving. The staff finally give in and persuade my family that letting me go back to Zurich is the best plan.

To be honest, no one could have realistically stopped me. I am 28 days sober; I have AA and I have a new chance at life.

On the afternoon of the 31st of March 2009, I leave the Priory and get a taxi to Heathrow airport in London. The flight to Zurich takes less than two hours and by early evening I am safely back in my home.

My new sober journey has started, and I really hope that I can make this a success.

I join Sika on 1st May 2009 and find I am back in a very stressful environment. The very first weekend I relapse and go out on a terrible drinking binge. I nearly throw all the hard work of the Priory, my family and myself away.

I manage to stop drinking about midnight on Sunday and go to bed. When the alarm goes on Monday morning, I seriously consider giving up and going drinking.

But finding strength from somewhere, I put myself into autopilot and manage to make it through the second week. At this point I resolve to do at least 90 days of sobriety to really give it a chance to work.

That 90 days turns to 180 days and that 180 days doubles and ends up with me receiving a "One year sober" coin from Alcoholics Anonymous. After that, I am voted chairman of the Saturday night AA meeting in Zurich, a position I hold for one year. I then hold several other service positions in AA over the next 2 years.

I have 3 years of sobriety and I start to believe I can make it work over the long term. I certainly still have a lot of stress at work, and I still worry about the future but at my core I know that I am now a sober person. I also have confidence that I have a higher power guiding me through life.

All I must do in the future, is as much good as possible to make up for all the bad things I have done in my life. If I can leave a small legacy of good things, then I will have done everything that has been asked of me and for that chance I will be forever grateful.

Chapter 13: Sobriety in the Long Term

Staying sober over the long term is not easy. For an alcoholic, it is the first two or three years that are most challenging. I attended AA meetings a lot during this period, and I received a lot of support. Even today with over 10 years sobriety, I still attend a meeting about once a week.

To be able to discuss your problem with someone who really understands you is the real strength of the AA movement and Tradition 3 "The only requirement for AA membership is a desire to stop drinking" is the tradition that convinced me that here is a fellowship where I truly belong.

Sobriety has fantastic benefits over the long term and my only regret is that I didn't get sober earlier. I have used what I learned in AA and the 12-step program in my fight to tackle my obesity. I have also used my faith in my AA higher power to come to terms with my cancer diagnosis and to accept the outcome, whatever that may be.

Life is a journey that always ends in death but if we put all our energy into improving ourselves and helping others then we will be moving in the right direction. At the end of the day if we all work together, we can also help the planet to survive and recover and fulfil our obligation to future generations.

I for one, thank my higher power for my experiences and hope he will be gentle with me as I move into old age.

Chapter 14: Final Thoughts

Apart from my first book ("Desperately Seeking Sex & Sobriety") I have written several other inspirational guides based on my 64 years' experience of life, alcoholism, obesity, cancer, redemption, and God.
Currently these are:
"How I Lost 30 Kilos (66 lbs) by Fasting"
"My Journey with Prostate Cancer"
"Is There a God or Not?"
And the trilogy:
"Fasting, Cancer & God"
Which is a compilation of the 3 short guides above.

These guides are designed to help you through any difficulties you are experiencing and give you the strength to improve your life and continue to survive and thrive.
My motto is "Get Sober, Get God, Do Good".
If you can do these 3 things, then I believe everything will work out alright for you.

Epilogue

I now live a sober life. I have been sober for over 10 years and I am very happy in this lifestyle. In the last 2 years I have lost the 30 kilos I had gained due to my alcoholism. I have moved from an obese weight to a healthy weight, and I feel so much better.

I was also recently diagnosed with aggressive prostate cancer, which I have decided to treat mainly with fasting rather than surgery or radiation.

My faith and trust in God have increased since he saved me from the alcoholism that was killing me. I don't know what God has in store for me in the future, but I do know that I will do his will as that is all there is.

I have no fear as I move towards the end of my life and if I have one day or 30+ years, I know I am living in God's grace, and I must accept his will.

I hope you have gained something from my story even if that is only the knowledge that you should never give up in the face of adversity.

Finally, I urge you to take these 3 steps to make the world a slightly better place:

Get Sober.
Get God.
Do Good.